Still Dancing

MARY McCONNELL

Still Dancing

LIFE CHOICES AND
CHALLENGES FOR WOMEN

HARBINGER HOUSE
Tucson   New York

HARBINGER HOUSE, INC.
Tucson, Arizona

© 1990 Mary McConnell
All Rights Reserved
Manufactured in the United States of America

∞ This book was printed on acid-free, archival-quality paper
Typeset in 11.5/14 Linotron 202 Weiss by Andresen Typographics
Designed by Kaelin Chappell

Excerpt from *Four Quartets,* copyright 1943 by T. S. Eliot and
renewed 1971 by Esme Valerie Eliot, reprinted by permission of
Harcourt Brace Jovanovich, Inc.

Excerpt from *Modern Man in Search of a Soul* by C. G. Jung,
reprinted by permission of Harcourt Brace Jovanovich, Inc.

Library of Congress Cataloging-in-Publication Data
McConnell, Mary, 1927-
    Still dancing : life choices and challenges for women / Mary
McConnell.
        p.   cm.
    Includes bibliographical references (pp. 244–254)
    ISBN 0-943173-54-X (alk. paper)
        1. Middle aged women—United States—Psychology—Case studies.
2. Self-actualization (Psychology)—Case studies.   I. Title.
HQ1059.5.U5M42   1990
305.24 ' 4—dc20   90-33639

To
Gwen
and to all women who are seeking
a woman's voice

CONTENTS

Preface   xi

Acknowledgments   xv

Some of the Women You Are About to Meet   3

ONE   Emily's Birthday Party   5

TWO   The Golden Years?   23

A Crucial Time   24

Responding to Crisis   25

How Young is "Young"?   26

Women Who "Have It All"   28

Society Won't Help Very Much   29

Breaking Out Is Hard to Do   30

Needed: A Better Image   31

The Good News   31

THREE   The Power of Aging: Bonuses as We Grow Older   33

The Freedom to Change   34

Adaptability   35

Acceptance of Differences   35

Spontaneity   36

Creativity   36

A Sense of Humor   41

Increased Tolerance for Stress 41
Greater Appreciation of Small Things 42
Liberation from Material Things 43
A Boost from Biology 44
The Survival Zone 45
Physical Aspects Can Be Modified 46
Self-Esteem 47
Sexuality 47
A Generation of Self-Starters 49
Good Social Skills 50
Important Connections 50
Optimism 52
Integration and Insight 53
Acquiring the Power 54

FOUR Surviving in a Difficult World:
Some Women Who Made It,
and Some Others Who Didn't 55
Caroline: A New Career 57
Kate: A Creative Woman Comes of Age 60
Anna: On the Forefront of Change 65
Elsie: A Triumph of the Spirit 71
Janet: Clouds in Paradise 73
Barbara: The Perils of a Perfect Marriage 76
Strategies to Outwit Aging 79

FIVE The Inward Journey 81
Am I Who Society Says I Am? 82
Do I Need a Personality Change? 83
Finding a New Purpose for Your Life 85
Taking Charge of Your Health 88
Building Self-Esteem 92
Finding Harmony with the Universe 100
Settling Unfinished Business with Parents 107
Counseling and Psychotherapy 109
Branching Out 116

SIX   Reaching Out to the World   117
Why the Old Roles Don't Work   118
Skills Women Need   121
Going Back to School   127
A Volunteer Career   132
Activism   134
Vocational Guidance   134
Community Services   137
Recreation   139
Adventure   140

SEVEN   Older Women in the Business World   144
Younger Workers Preferred   146
Discrimination and the Law   152
So Now What Do We Do?   153
The Price of "Making It": Miriam's Story   160
Women Can Succeed!   162

EIGHT   Special Relationships   164
The Men in Our Lives   164
Our Adult Children   177
Our Aging Parents   191

NINE   Relating to Our Doctors   199
Medical Care   199
Mental Health Care   205

TEN   Reclaiming Our Heritage   211
Where Wrinkles Mean Power and Influence   212
A Chinese Woman Talks about Aging   215
The Strength of Jewish Women   218
Native American Women   220
Ancient Goddesses   224
Can We Regain Some of Our Power?   228

ELEVEN Reflections   229
        On Money and Power   229
        On Children   230
        On Happiness   230
        On Sex as Trivial Pursuit   231
        On Continued Learning   231
        On Getting It All Together   232
        On Real Old Age: The Painful Look Ahead   235
        But in the Meantime   237
        Our Contribution to Society   240

        Bibliography   244

PREFACE

Turning sixty sneaks up on you, like a difficult guest you know is coming—but since the guest's arrival is far in the future and you're not looking forward to it anyway, you postpone planning for the occasion. And suddenly Sixty knocks at the door.

It's fun getting into the movies at a senior discount. At three dollars a throw, I can see every movie in town. It reminds me of when I was a kid and could see the latest Tarzan matinee for a dime. But then I began to wonder whether society might be discounting me in other ways, too.

Just how much of a decline is there in middle age? In what areas? Is there anything we can do to counteract it? I had to find out. I talked to women in these years of late middle age—fifty to seventy-plus—and to psychologists and other professionals who work with them. It became apparent that people have very different reactions to aging. Many react with illness and depression, while others respond with new verve and purpose.

Growing older in a culture that has been solidly youth-oriented for at least thirty years is a vital issue. Just at the time when people need new identities and new meaning for their lives, they face more difficulties in acquiring them.

Are we like athletes running a marathon? The runners dig in. The first few miles are run swiftly, then a little slower. Suddenly the runners experience an almost overwhelming feeling of fatigue and muscle ache. One by one they "hit the wall." But the race is not over. In fact, the last six miles and 385 yards are the most important part. Those who are winners will get past "the wall," test the limits of their endurance, and run through their agony to a triumphant finish. This may be what life is all about: those last six miles.

When I turned sixty, I felt I had hit the wall and it was time to begin this book. I talked with women who have experienced the difficulties and losses that life brings. Many of these women have made it. They may not have achieved success in any worldly sense, but they feel good about themselves and have positive goals in their lives. Some women who have always had confidence and energy remained undaunted by age. I concentrated on women who have been tested by the life situations that aging often brings—illness, death of a spouse, divorce, employment problems, financial loss. These women coped with these difficulties with just average assets—no wealth, power, talent, or social prestige; and only a few had striking beauty. If they could do it, perhaps we all can.

Since we also learn from those who did *not* make it, I talked with women whose lives are less than satisfying. Some have escaped the fear of aging in alcohol, codependency, and other addictions. I also interviewed professionals who work with troubled women.

I contacted some of the women after hearing about their struggles and triumphs. Others got in touch with me after hearing about my work. We talked about their expectations of aging, their experiences, events of the past that shaped their personalities, the obstacles they encountered as older women, and the methods of coping they found helpful. I also inquired about any positive qualities they had discovered as they aged, and we talked about their observations about today's society. I asked them if they had any advice for younger women. I used nondirective interview techniques to encourage their considerable spontaneity.

I tuned in to the implications on aging that I heard in conversations with people socially and in professional and other meetings. I absorbed comments heard on the popular television shows that feature such material. I read previous research on this subject, and I spoke with professionals who work with people in the generation now over fifty. The more I talked with people, the more I realized how important it is to explore the subject of aging.

What happens after you hit the wall? What is life like on the other side? It is my hope that this book will help women hit the wall fearlessly and complete the race with victory!

ACKNOWLEDGMENTS

I am deeply grateful to the special women who shared their personal struggles with me and articulately expressed their insights about growing older. And I appreciate the women, and men, who contributed their professional observations as well. I would like to thank all the people I interviewed, including those I can't acknowledge individually because they chose not to use their real names.

I would like to give Anna Cullinan—her real name—special mention, although she is not around to see it. Anna died from her cancer in 1989, but is still alive in the minds of the many people whose lives she touched. Anna was one of the first women I interviewed. Articulate and insightful, she got my research off to a marvelous start. I soon realized I was indeed onto something worth sharing with the world.

Special love and thanks go to Jeanne Mellinger, a psychologist who specializes in gerontology. Jeanne teaches at George Mason University in Virginia and has published research in this field. She contributed important support as a friend while also providing me with research information and contacts.

I am grateful to Martha Gore, my agent, who appreciated the importance of the concept of this book and worked to make it a reality. I am grateful to the editor and staff at Harbinger House for seeing the potential of this book in its early stages. Special thanks to Ricky Bourque, whose insightful editing contributed so much to the final product. Typist and friend Hazel Froud helped at a crucial moment, as did Elizabeth Shaw. John McConnell, my son, untangled a glitch in my computer, when the computer company couldn't, so that the manuscript could proceed on schedule. I wish to send love to my mother, Rachel Fair, who may not be up to reading this entire book, but whose own valiant spirit has influenced me.

Since a writer writes out of life experience, I feel a special gratitude to those who enriched my life during the work on this book. Helen Briggs believed in the book when it was yet a vision and I had not written a page. Writer-friend Maggie Wahl encouraged me early on as well, with both friendship and literary suggestions. Jann Kennedy was another source of support throughout the entire project. Anyone who has undertaken an ambitious project such as this understands how vital it is to have your family behind you. My sons Robert and Harry were always encouraging, and a medal should go to my husband, Ross, for his never-failing love and support. He has my deepest gratitude and appreciation.

Still Dancing

SOME OF THE WOMEN
YOU ARE ABOUT TO MEET

Carla Whitcomb, who just turned fifty and feels betrayed
by age

Doris Reed, at twenty a showgirl at the Schubert Theatre in
New York; at seventy-four, a poet; reflects on life at
eighty-five

Anna Cullinan, mother, politician, and humorist, who set
out to find out how men get their power so she could
achieve some for herself

Dr. Grace Kaiser, who went from delivering babies to a
new career in writing after a personal catastrophe

Rachel Zane, activist at seventy

Anita Romero, who talks frankly about older women in the
workplace

Sarah Lerner, a traveler and philosopher at eighty-four, who
offers insights on women's difficulties

Barrie Ryan, younger than fifty, who teaches "The Gifts of
Age," a unique course for men and women over fifty

Caroline Anderson, former housewife of the fifties, who
struggled to find a new career as a journalist

Kate Maxwell, a preacher's daughter during the Depression, who overcame obstacles and developed her creativity

Ruth Gardner, recently retired university teacher, who is
taking My Year, to reflect and find her true direction

Eileen Feuerbach, now completing her Ph.D. and starting a professional career at age sixty-nine

Gay Frank, who found enrichment through travel to exotic places

Cindy Ellis, thirty-six, who reveals a hidden problem between women of late middle age and their adult children—and tells how she deals with it

Jean Chaudhuri, a Creek Indian, who reveals the source of her strength: the training and inspiration of her traditional culture

CHAPTER ONE

Emily's Birthday Party

Emily lifted her teacup for another sip of fragrant warmth. Lacy rosebuds and fragile vines encircled the translucent china. "Oh, if life could be as rounded and soothing as this cup of tea," Emily reflected.

"Life can go either way," she mused. "A woman on her sixtieth birthday is at a turning point. To be this age is to see your past stretched out in one direction and a suddenly limited future extending in another." The image of the shorter span ahead called for another sip of the hot jasmine tea.

"Really, Emily, sixty is quite young." Dorothy stirred milk and sugar in her tea, the way her British parents had taught her so long ago.

"Dorothy is steadying, good," thought Emily. "I need her today."

At eighty-five, Dorothy is alone, fighting ill health, but her spirit is strong and eyes are bright; and the older she grows, the more insightful her poetry becomes.

Anne entered the room and poured a cup of tea. Anne is thirty-five, a professional dancer. Her brown hair is braided into a long plait, a simple counterbalance to the drama of her high cheekbones, profound brown eyes, her honest, serene beauty.

"What's it like to be sixty, Emily? You look great! You must feel as though you've 'arrived.'"

"Arrived, yes," laughed Emily. "But arrived at what? Didn't Gertrude Stein say, 'When you get there, there isn't any there there'? I feel as young as ever, but something has changed—something rather important. I've been asked to take early retirement at the school. They're dissolving the Latin department. It's a dead language, they say. But *I'm* not dead. I still have a lot to give to the world. I'm a better teacher than I ever was. 'Tempus fugit,' they say. 'No one studies Latin anymore.'"

"I know that must hurt," Anne sympathized. "Actually, it frightens me," she added. "I know my days as a dancer are numbered, and I've thought I've been securing my future by studying archaeology at the university. But by the time I get my Ph.D.—which I'll need to get a job—I wonder if I'll be considered over the hill?"

"Things may change by then," Emily answered. "I'm hoping I can change things for myself now. But, you know, I've been through so much. I hope I can let go of some of the pain my generation experienced. If I can learn something from it all, then I should be able to concentrate on my assets."

"Pain?" Anne hadn't realized that under Emily's air of poise and confidence there was suffering.

"Those of us who are sixty today started out in the

Depression, the big one in the 1930s that had men standing on street corners, desperate and ashamed, selling apples and pencils. I used to ache with sadness when I saw my mother hand them a few pennies.

"I was too young to remember everything about the Depression," Emily continued, "but I did learn at an early age to do without. And our parents bore the effects of the Depression for the rest of their lives. They never wanted to spend money on anything they thought was 'foolishness.'"

"That's right," Dorothy agreed. "For years we were terrified of spending money. To this day, I still wind string into balls."

"Even though no one uses string anymore," laughed Anne.

Dorothy tipped her head. "You just never know when you might need it."

Quietly, Emily reflected on these difficult years. "The Depression experience may have affected me far more than I realized. I can remember being talked out of things I wanted. There was a ruffled dress with big dots that Shirley Temple wore. I wanted that dress in the worst way!"

"Yes, I remember that dress," Doris said. "They used it on the Shirley Temple dolls."

Emily continued, "And Shirley had a big barrel, scooped out so she could sit in it and pretend it was an airplane. My father made one for me. He scooped it out by hand so I could rock and sing, too—just like Shirley. I guess I did get things I wanted sometimes, just so long as they didn't cost any money.

"Later, I wanted cashmere sweaters. There was a kind of caste system at high school. The wealthy girls wore cashmeres, and the rest of us wore the ordinary wool kinds. Remember those loose sweaters that we buttoned down the back?"

"And you think the way *I* dress is wild," Anne teased.

"Oh, we had our crazy styles, too," Emily laughed. "Our dirty saddle shoes, for instance. We had to go out and muddy them up a bit before we could wear them to school. To wear them shiny and new would have been a disgrace."

"Just like our blue jeans," said Anne.

"And then there was 'the poorhouse.' I never saw it or even knew if it existed outside of a Dickens novel—but people kept talking about it. My parents saved for me to go to college. But all through school, I had an awful fear that we would end up in the poorhouse before I could get to the university!"

"You must understand our fear," Dorothy said. "The 1920s were free and easy. My friends and I bobbed our hair and threw away our corsets and danced like fools to the Charleston. But the crash that followed was devastating, and we never trusted frivolity again."

"As a child, I didn't actually feel poor," Emily explained. "Everyone I knew had the same modest standards. We didn't know about affluence. We didn't have television to tell us about the lives of the rich and famous."

"That's right," Dorothy said. "Prosperity was having enough to eat, and wealth was having dishes that matched or glasses that hadn't started out as jelly glasses."

"Life was good," Emily continued. "It was innocent and free, in its way. But as I look back, it also was limiting in its scope. It didn't allow us the freedom to think about personal goals and choices."

"But with Depression memories, you'd think careers would be all-important," said Anne.

"Yes, you'd think so," Emily replied. "I don't know why people didn't seem to have higher ambitions then. Perhaps it was because most middle-class young people couldn't afford college, although the Second World War was to change that for men. In those days it was enough to work, earn a living, raise a family, and just be a respectable member of the community. And we young girls knew that Prince Charming was going to worry about all those financial matters, anyway. We just had to concentrate on being worthy of him, pretty, charming, virginal. It seems so silly, in retrospect. What we *needed* to pay attention to was the life choices we could make."

Anne sympathized. "Choices are so important for a woman."

"Yes," said Dorothy. "Today's young women scrutinize every choice, making sure they are on track—their personal track, that is, not society's."

"Didn't you have any choices?" asked Anne.

"Oh, I suppose we did have choices," Emily admitted. "We just didn't pay much heed to them. Young women were educated along with the men; but still, they were expected to follow traditional feminine roles. Those of us who managed to go on to college could prepare for a career. But when we met Mr. Right, we were expected to modify our goals to fit into our new careers as housewives and mothers.

"I suppose we were learning to adapt to society. Without realizing it, society was already expanding and changing. If only we had had television! We would have known more about the different ways women can live."

"Today," said Anne, "we have so many role models and television examples and peers that it's mind boggling. We may suffer, actually, from too *many* choices. My parents told me I could be anything I wanted to be. But along with offering the choices, I wish my parents had warned me about the limits. Not social limits, but the limits of human endurance. I dance, I care for my child, take care of my home, and I study at the university. I'm so weary all the time. I sometimes wonder if I'm doing *any* of it well."

"True," Emily reflected. "Women have always had a difficult position. You just can't be all things to all people, and we haven't recognized that."

Dorothy recalled her earlier years. "Choices? Careers? Darlings, in my day no woman aimed for a career."

"How sad." Anne reflected on how repressed these women, her friends, had been at her age. "But at least you were given some respect for being a housewife."

"That's true. But oh, how poorly prepared some of us were," said Dorothy. Her family had been wealthy, and she was raised in the British manner as a "proper" lady. "I wasn't taught how to cook. We had servants for that. My sisters and I were taught how to embroider, to play the piano, and dance the waltz. What we *weren't* taught is how to take care of ourselves in a rough-and-tumble world."

"Not everyone had your advantages, Dorothy."

"That's very true. Many women in my generation were farmers' wives, and they got a very thorough training in survival early in life. Parents and children worked side by side to keep alive. They were not quite so bound by Victorian tradition. But don't underestimate the Victorian influence on *all* family life during that time. It created a home that was dominated by the parents, the father in particular. Children were held at a distance. They were considered inherently wild and in need of constant discipline and training."

"Dorothy," Anne asked, "what did you expect out of life?"

"It was all going to be so terribly romantic. Life was all about finding Heathcliff and living happily ever after. What actually happened was something else. My husband was an alcoholic who disappointed me in every way. I divorced him and supported our children by myself. Without any career training, my life turned out to be quite rough indeed."

"What about your mother?" Anne wondered.

"The Victorian romantic idea ruined my mother. Her life with a difficult, authoritarian husband broke her spirit. I wrote a poem about her. After she died, I found it as I was going through her treasures. I still have it." Dorothy reached into a drawer and brought out a faded sheet of paper.

*The Lower Drawer**

Tinted miniature of a maiden.
Pale eyes not yet awake, flower cheeks,
ampule of violet in lemon wood,
pearl barrette to catch the tendrils
at the nape of the milky column.

Dead dreams buried
in the lower drawer.
A baptism for madness.

The three women were silent for a moment. Then, "What about you, Emily?" Anne asked softly. "What did you expect love would bring?"

"Love, in the person of Prince Charming, was going to take care of everything. The young girls of my generation believed we'd get married and live happily ever after, too— just like in the fairy tales. To catch the prince became our only goal. We may not have had information about the direction women's roles might take—but we did have role models for looking gorgeous!"

"Oh, yes. The thirties and forties were the Golden Years of Hollywood," Dorothy recalled. "Those were the days of Betty Grable, Lana Turner, Veronica Lake."

Emily smiled. "Veronica Lake, where are you now? In the forties, high school girls had long hair—preferably blonde—that cascaded over their shoulders with a wave

*This poem was written by Doris Reed when she was seventy-four years old.

covering one eye. We *all* wanted to be mysterious and glamorous, just like Veronica. We piled on pancake makeup until all facial flaws were concealed. Of course, a lot of our natural beauty got concealed, too, but it wasn't until years later that we realized that. We even plucked our eyebrows into twin arches so we'd always look startled. Nothing was too much for beauty. We thought beauty was our power. But as it turned out, the power that counts in life is all psychological and mental. No one told us that in the forties, though."

"Didn't your parents encourage you to be anything more than beautiful?" asked Anne.

"They encouraged us to do well in school, yes. But in other ways, we were repressed. I can still remember my father saying, 'Children should be seen and not heard.' Worse, 'Spare the rod and spoil the child.' What was considered important was to have the bottoms of our kitchen pans shiny and bright and our floors gleaming with wax. 'Cleanliness is next to godliness,' we were told. I remember wondering secretly if God really addressed himself to the bottoms of our pans."

"A lot of platitudes," Anne commented.

"You know," Emily continued, "I think the most damaging ones were 'Pride goeth before a fall' and its corollary, 'The bigger they come the harder they fall.' They seemed to make sense at the time. Later, though, it seemed that just the opposite was true. The people with self-esteem became the leaders of our generation. That group didn't often include women."

"That's terrible," Anne said. "I hope your therapist helped you unravel that."

"Therapist? Freud was coming into popularity in the forties, and many people did get analyzed. But most families held to the belief that getting psychological help was somehow shameful. I remember one time when I was crying about my problems. My parents said, 'Keep a stiff upper lip.'"

"Another platitude."

"That's true, but it did give me a knowledge that without outside support, I would just have to learn to face my problems and cope with them."

"Yes," Dorothy agreed. "Especially after we saw that Heathcliff and Prince Charming weren't going to do it for us."

"I don't mean that I was always so rational," said Emily. "My expectations put a terrible strain on my marriage. Poor Fred has always been just a human being, like me. He has enough to do, just working out his own life. I shouldn't have expected so much from him in the beginning.

"I remember how comparatively liberated young men were in those days. At home it was, 'Emily, set the table,' and 'Sit up straight, dear.' But with my brother and my boy cousins, I learned to swing on long ropes from trees, jump in the haymow in a barn. I learned how to break free from a woman's life."

"Haymow!"

"That was on my grandmother's farm. At home we had sidewalks. I used to rollerskate up and down the block, my skate key swinging on a ribbon around my neck as I moved along. Sometimes I stumbled over the cracks between the sidewalk slabs. 'Step on a crack and you break your mother's back.' Remember that one? No, I guess not. Anyway, I was carefree in a way that children can't be today."

"I could never let my Carol out like that," Anne said. "The neighborhood just isn't safe."

"I know. But in those days we didn't know about rape, drugs, urban crime. So, in some ways, we did have freedom.

"Then another major event occurred to shape our lives—World War II. Adults and children alike agonized over the hardships of our men in battle and the terror and uncertainties of life in Europe."

"And it was a second time of doing without," added Dorothy. "Again it was a time of sacrifice, of living for the future. The sacrifices on the home front were small but ever-present. Sugar, meat, automobile tires, and gasoline were rationed severely. I remember squeezing pellets of yellow dye into white margarine to look like the butter that was restricted. But war or no war, glamour was still in. We couldn't get silk stockings, so we put makeup on our legs and drew penciled lines down the back to look like stocking seams. The men had Betty Grable pin-ups on their locker doors, and we wanted them to remember us as being attractive, too."

"In 1943 I entered high school," said Emily. "Like so many other girls of the time, I said goodbye to Fred, the handsome older 'boy next door' who enlisted in the Navy on his eighteenth birthday. Fred was my brother's best friend, and I had decided when I was eight years old that he was *my* Prince Charming.

"During those war years," Emily continued, "women did without their men, the very people who were going to give them the love and freedom they longed for. Their boy-friends went to strange-sounding places like Guadalcanal and Iwo Jima. Many of them never came back. On the home front, we rolled bandages, we knit warm socks for the boys overseas. Mostly, though, we wrote letters and prayed for their survival."

Softly, Dorothy hummed a popular song from that era. "I'll walk alone, without your love and your kisses to guide me . . ." Emily smiled. "All the songs then were about lone-liness and unfulfilled love.

"My older sister married her boyfriend before he went overseas," Emily continued. "There was a terrific rush to get married, to grab whatever happiness you could before war had a chance to destroy it."

"Why not just make love?" Anne asked.

"Make love? Some did, I know. But for most of us, virginity was our key to a good marriage. 'What nice man would want used goods?' people said. I suppose for the men, marriage was a way of knowing someone was home waiting for them, possibly with a child who would be their posterity.

"Many women followed their husbands from camp to camp, rather than endure long separations. My sister Ellen stayed home, but she did follow the trend to go all-out for the war effort. She got a job as an electrician's assistant for a ship manufacturer."

"I remember hearing of Rosie the Riveter," Anne said.

"Those working women had difficult jobs, but they were well paid. And suddenly, for the first time in their lives, they learned to be independent, to plan their lives and their finances. Their self-confidence grew. It was a terrible blow for them to lose their jobs when the men came home from the war."

"But they didn't *have* to stop working," Anne exclaimed. "I wouldn't have!"

"Oh, but they *did*. Women were dismissed without question. They were told it wasn't right to take a job away from a serviceman."

"That's so unfair!"

"Yes, it was," answered Dorothy. "But it was just the way life was. That's not to say that the women were always happy to be back home. Many marriages fell apart when the man, who had been raised from birth to be in charge, came home to a woman who now had some take-charge experience herself. But for most young women, home life was seen as the refuge they needed. It was the source of their happiness."

"When Fred came home," said Emily, "he entered college on the GI Bill. We dated for four years while we worked toward our degrees, his in business administration, mine in education. Finally we graduated, and two weeks later I married Fred in a flurry of satin and lace. Our wedding was so romantic, so beautiful. It was my dream come true!

"We were so much in love! And the superconventional years of the fifties were really such fun! I made curtains for the living room and hung a dozen plants to cover up the bareness of our first home, bought with a VA loan out in a brand-new subdivision west of town. I had a garden, and we entertained friends on Saturday nights at our backyard barbecue. Soon the children arrived, and they added to our delight.

"Prosperity had finally happened for the first time in our lives. Fred bought me an automatic washing machine (no more rollers to squeeze clothes through!) and a dryer to replace the long clotheslines. Some of my friends even got dishwashers. Advertising cooperated by bombarding us with pictures of glamorous women at home, happily surrounded by work-saving gadgets."

Emily fell silent, remembering. The shadow of a frown appeared between her brows.

"Then what?" asked Anne.

"After a few years, I began to feel isolated. I wanted to go back to teaching. Many of my friends were beginning to feel restless, too. But people—our mothers, mothers-in-law, and other housewives—were criticizing women who worked. Dr. Spock added to our guilt. He was our child-care expert whose book on baby care gave us the information we needed out there in the suburbs, alone with our babies. He insisted that a mother needed to be home for the first five years of a child's life. Since birth-control pills hadn't been developed yet, our families tended to be large, and those five years stretched into many. So many, in fact, that we forget what we started out to do."

"Imagine a pediatrician having such influence!"

"Remember, Anne, that we were in nuclear families, without the relatives who would have provided advice in the past. Dr. Spock was right, though. Children do need their mothers. And watching an infant develop is one of life's main pleasures. We felt very needed, very useful. Motherhood was our career.

"Funny," Emily mused, "for such an important career we should have gotten recognition. Instead, it seemed to go the other way. In my case, I had no opportunity to use my education and I felt more subjugated to my husband than I had ever thought possible."

"So you didn't plan it that way?" Anne asked.

"No, indeed. I really thought that Fred and I were equals. He earned the money, something a man could do much more successfully than a woman in those days. And I had the all-important job of raising the children. I don't know how it happened, but somehow men got to be more dominant. Perhaps it was because the world was giving so much prestige to their achievements. What a mother does is invisible. I began to realize that when people found Fred's position as a sales manager far more noteworthy than my raising a son who adjusted well to school and had a happy life.

"Perhaps, too, we women lacked so much mental stimulation that we began to lose our ability to think for ourselves. Even today, in my generation, a wife who expresses a radically different opinion from her husband is looked on askance. My neighbor used to vote the same way her husband voted. 'If I don't, what's the use of voting? Our votes will cancel each other.' I was never that bad—but I wasn't doing all that well, either.

"It was truly a 'split-level trap,' as a book by that name suggested. I'll never forget a scene in the movie, *Diary of a Mad Housewife*. The poor woman was being bullied by her husband, who was issuing orders about how perfect things had to be when his boss came for dinner.

"We were in a bind. Yet you must give us credit for giving our children lots of freedom."

"And we appreciate it," Anne said.

Dorothy spoke up. "Women have been told for generations that their work is important, but they're seldom treated as if it were. I think we're told that our work is vital so we'll keep on doing it. The men certainly don't want to."

"It was worse than just not being recognized," said Emily. "Suddenly there seemed to be a wave of reaction against this woman of the fifties. After all, she had no outside job, yet she wielded so much power in the newly emerging consumer marketplace. Worst of all, she had so much influence over the children. Philip Wylie brought it all to a head in his book, *The Generation of Vipers*. He called Mom 'a parasitic viper who chews gum, eats bonbons, and plays bridge with the stupid voracity of a hammerhead shark.'"

Anne laughed. "People took that seriously?"

"The book was a bestseller!"

"Not only that," Dorothy recalled, "but the new generation of pampered children . . ."

"I beg your pardon!" Anne bristled.

"That's just how people began to see them," Emily answered. "These perfectly raised, nurtured children were not growing up problem free. They were hyperactive, shy, schizoid, homosexual, aggressive, they stole hubcaps. And with Mother around all the time, everyone assumed that she was to blame. After all, hadn't she poured all her education and energy into the job of raising these children?

"So once again women were thrown at the mercy of men—as the experts were then. Fathers were not only off the hook; they were convinced that they must spend more time with their sons to combat the mothers' possessiveness.

A mother who was unhappy with her role in life was said to be 'neurotic, rejecting the feminine role.'"

"I didn't know you felt that way about psychologists, Emily."

"Today psychologists have a more enlightened view. And certainly a woman who doesn't like the traditional role is no longer considered unbalanced.

"It took Betty Friedan and her book, *The Feminine Mystique*, published in 1963, to give us the support we needed. Ms. Friedan saw the damage that years of oppression and economic dependence had done to women."

"Hurrah! At last your troubles were over!"

"Not quite," Emily answered. "Now it was all right for mothers to work. But decades of staying home, of having low self-esteem and little mental stimulation, had taken its toll. I hadn't had a job interview for almost twenty years. I did go back to school, and I got my Ph.D. in the classical languages, but it was many years before I was really qualified to apply for a teaching job. I never did and never *will* recoup those lost years professionally. And now I'm sixty years old, and I'm being asked to retire. It's as if the timing has always been wrong for me!"

"A lot of us aren't raised for the real world," said Dorothy. "We are raised for a world somebody else thinks it is."

"Do you feel that way, Anne?"

"Well, I don't know yet. Women my age have been told they can do it all—have lofty careers, raise a family, and still be creative and interesting. I find the work world is still male dominated, and I can't seem to find the help I need with my home and family. I'm beginning to doubt the premise."

"That's interesting," Emily commented. "I remember when I went back to school how difficult it was to juggle everything. Household help was easier to find and less expensive, too, in those days. Women don't choose domestic work now."

"Emily, don't forget the impact that Vietnam had on our lives," Dorothy reminded her. "I lost a grandson in battle, and another grandson to drugs. He's alive out there somewhere, we don't know where. I guess he's still looking for another high."

"I know, Dorothy." Emily put her arm around her friend's shoulder. "It's a tragedy. The events that shaped my life, and complicated it, brought disaster to yours. During the Vietnam years, people began to question the Establishment. I was discontent, but I felt trapped within society's bounds. At the same time, my children, the baby boomers, felt free to rebel against all of society. How poorly our needs have been met by the basic institutions we used to revere. Street drugs became part of the everyday lives of young people. Many, like your grandson, never recovered from the drug scene. And as teenagers stressed parents to the limits, divorces became more common. It was a difficult time to be a parent."

"I wish I had realized that at the time," Dorothy said. "I know now that I didn't give my daughter the support she needed then. I had nothing but criticism about the way her children were behaving."

"We were a generation caught in the middle," Emily said. "We were parents who insisted on the traditional values we had grown up with, and our children proclaimed their right to do away with them. I think it did teach us something important, though; and that is, to question the way things are. To seek new answers. For me, the drug world holds no appeal; but I don't have to keep pleasing everyone, either."

"Well, now that we're in the 1990s, things have settled down," said Anne. "Women can live the kind of lives they want."

"Yes, and I am very glad for that," Emily agreed. "But again, that fact is forcing me to make still another turn-around. It was so hard for me to get back into the work world, and now suddenly I'm out of a job again. There *are* new opportunities for women, but that seems to translate to *young* women. Again, I seem to be in the right place at the wrong time.

"But I do still have Fred," Emily continued. "So many of my friends are alone now. Their husbands felt they had missed out on the sexual revolution and they wanted to get on the new bandwagon. So Women's Liberation liberated men, too. At least, in the old days a wife had a certain status and security. And here we are, so many of us, with no husbands and no career, or only moderately developed careers because of our more restricted past."

"What a stab in the back!" Anne said.

"I think there is a new pressure to be young and glamorous," Dorothy observed. "It's almost like it was in the Veronica Lake days you were talking about. And I think the new glamour girls look a little bit like Veronica. It's that long blonde hair, I guess. Only this time, they don't cover one eye. Both eyes are open, alert to career opportunities."

"That's right!" Emily laughed. "They do look similar, but today they're more aggressive. They even appear on TV talk shows."

"Well, Emily, at least you are free now to do what you want with your life. No more Dr. Spock or children or shiny pans!"

"Yes, I am free. But many of my 'sisters' are not. My neighbor, Jane, is raising two of her grandchildren. Her daughter got a divorce and had a breakdown. Then there is Mother, who is getting more frail every day. I don't know how much longer she'll be able to live alone. With women living longer than ever, some women my age are actually caring for four generations at once: their aging parents, children, grandchildren, themselves. I am lucky to have the comparative freedom to explore my options."

"Yes," Dorothy agreed, "I dread having to impose on my own daughter, knowing how difficult it will be for her. She has already raised a family and—like you—she deserves some freedom."

"This is scary," said Anne.

"Yes, it is," Dorothy and Emily touched her hand.

"Society has wobbled in its expectations of women, like a drunken acrobat on a pole," Emily said. "It's time we women learned to turn things around!"

The teapot was empty. The women embraced and left the room.

CHAPTER TWO

The Golden Years?

"I can truly be myself for the first time," says Areta Johnson, a fifty-five-year-old psychiatric nurse.

"Now that I'm seventy, I feel more empowered than when I was twenty," says Arizona Gray Panthers director Rachel Zane. "I feel as if there isn't anything I can't accomplish, there isn't anyone I can't approach."

But other women express a startlingly different opinion.

"At sixty, women hit a big drop," laments Amy Adams, sixty-two. "I feel that I have something to say now, but no one wants to listen."

"I seldom see a happy woman in the fifty- to seventy-five-year age range," a psychiatrist notes.

Carla Whitcomb, an elementary school teacher who just turned fifty, feels betrayed. "I look at the annual class photos, and I watch myself aging. The photographers give me the pictures every year, so I can't ignore the changes. I feel the same as always, but I look like my mother."

Who is right? What's the real story about being over fifty? Is it a positive or a negative experience—or both? Inherently it is one of the most difficult times of a woman's life. Yet it also is a time of life that has a special kind of potential, and even a new power.

What factors lead to successful living for a woman in middle age? What are the fulfilled women doing that the others aren't? Have they had easier lives than their sisters whose lives are in decline? Most of the women you will meet in this book have experienced deprivation, loss, and difficulty. All have learned to accept change. And all have developed special qualities that helped them continue to grow and find new meanings in their lives.

A CRUCIAL TIME

There is so much at stake today. Only a few generations ago, men and women died soon after their youngest child reached maturity. There was no opportunity for late-in-life crisis. Now, a woman of fifty can expect to live for thirty or forty more years—far too long a time to spend in despondency.

Maturity is not unlike adolescence. It is a confusing time of life. Our faces, our bodies, all aspects of our lives are changing and we feel out of control. At late middle age, the look backward can be disconcerting. The sorrows and joys of the years gone by are intermingled so intrinsically that it's difficult to separate the happy times from the sad. As painful as life may have been, in perspective it also is beautiful. The years ahead are fewer than those that have already passed. This is frightening; the adolescent can always say, "There's time."

Growing older and changing one's life role are subjects we approach with fear. Yet by some time in their fifties, most people have begun to search for personal meaning. This search is the major developmental task of age. Growth is still available at sixty or seventy or even eighty. However, what a woman acquires in self-knowledge, exploring alternatives, and finding new life directions in late middle age will determine how well she copes with continued aging. Shirley Campbell reports this fact in her research.

RESPONDING TO CRISIS

A woman finds a lump on her breast, and she rushes to the doctor. Whether benign or malignant, the lump symbolizes the dreadful knowledge that life is limited. At the office, another woman receives a memo about early retirement. She overhears a young colleague mumble something about "getting rid of the deadwood." A woman's husband leaves her for another woman, one who seems full of youthful energy. The new wife wears glasses, too—but they're not bifocals.

Be glad for a crisis! It is a call for action. A crisis can provide the impetus to reassess one's path in life, one's attitudes and goals. The women who seem most vital in their later years often are women who have been divorced, widowed, or have suffered some similar crisis in late middle age that got them moving in new ways.

But even without a major crisis, women need to acknowledge that a new phase of life is brewing. Unless we take the trouble—and pain—to examine our lives, we delay forming the attitudes and coping skills we need when the going gets tougher. People with pleasant lives and few difficulties have not had to develop the ability to cope with the negative. When they are faced with a serious loss—the death of a husband or a heart attack at seventy—they are devastated. Be glad, then, for the crises that come to you when you are only fifty or sixty. They will strengthen you for the long haul.

HOW YOUNG IS "YOUNG"?

Fifty and sixty and even seventy are not old. Sarah Lerner, an eighty-four-year-old world traveler, says, "Sixty is young. Oh, what I could do if I were only sixty!" Many women look and feel young at these ages. Mary Ann Goff, a social worker, claims that the whole structure of what we call midlife is beginning to change. "There are so many of us who are in our fifties and sixties who are alive and alert and have tremendous talents to offer. What do we do with these people?"

What indeed? There lies the obstacle for today's woman. At the moment the woman is most prepared to take a place in the world, she may be the least encouraged by society to find it. She knows she is young, but no one else seems to know it. While over fifty is still young, it is not "young" in the way our youth-oriented society means. "I wish I had known this before," says Beth Ferris.

At fifty-four, Beth feels young. She thought she could renew her career any time she chose. The time came, and she discovered that employers were reluctant to hire her. Beth didn't realize that society's perception of her would differ so much from the way she felt and saw herself. Had she known sooner, she would never have permitted a family move to take her away from her career. Or perhaps she would have returned to the university and gotten her degree.

There is a lot of truth in the old saying, "You're only as

old as you feel." The mind is powerful, and thinking young will keep you young—as a general rule. But, like many platitudes, it doesn't come to grips with the identity crisis that can come at late middle age. Even though we may feel young, think young, and look young (or at least younger than our age), we won't pass for twenty-eight. Society may expect us to take a back seat; and younger people may say, "You had your chance."

What does it mean to "feel young"? Most people feel young some of the time. At eighty-four, Doris Reed feels young during those moments when night turns into day and she first awakens.

> At night on my old lady's bed
> I lie with child dreams.
> At first stretch comes memory.
> Youth rescues me each night.
> Old age recaptures me at dawn.

What do we do when we no longer feel young? And what makes us feel young? Is it health? At fifty-seven, Anna Cullinan is cheerful and smiling. But Anna has bone cancer. Still, she has an inner vitality that she shares with others. "You can die from cancer for years," she exclaims. "How much better to live each day to its fullest!"

Perhaps it's wisdom. We could say, "You're young as long as you've got the inner spirit of a wise woman."

"Just keep busy and you won't notice age." This is another platitude that contains some truth. "I hardly have time to read the newspaper," say many happy older people. It is easier to grow and feel satisfaction when you can expand into the community. However, endless activity also can be a defense against honestly facing late middle age. Sometimes we need to step back and consider our real needs before plunging ahead with activity. Some women who have spent their lives on a treadmill of activity feel they have missed the mark. Activities tend to perpetuate themselves and may not leave time for thinking about their true meaning.

WOMEN WHO "HAVE IT ALL"

Some of the women whose lives are thriving at sixty seem to have been blessed with more than average self-confidence and ability and a minimum of obstacles. Marilyn Bernard, now seventy-six, was one of those women. When she was sixty, Marilyn would have seen little need for reflection and reassessment of goals. Her basic needs and her life situation meshed well. As a young girl, she had received an unusual amount of career encouragement from her father, and she was one of the first women to obtain a Ph.D. in psychology at the local university—a remarkable achievement for the time. For many years she worked as a clinical psychologist. Marilyn was free from the many identity problems that most women have in our culture. She never bought into the idea that marriage and family represented "the feminine role." Physical beauty was not one of her values, so she didn't fear gray hairs and wrinkles. When she was forced to retire at sixty-five, she found another job and continued working for several years.

Marilyn's first life crisis came at seventy-one when she had a stroke. No longer able to work, Marilyn lost the main focus of her life. Alone, with no family and few friends to lend support, she finds life confining and depressing. "I will never recover from this physical and psychological blow," she declares.

Grace Kaiser is another woman who "had it all." As an obstetrician in rural Pennsylvania, she delivered most of the babies born to Amish women in her community. Often she traveled at night to attend them at home deliveries. Dr.

Kaiser had a supportive husband who helped to raise their four children.

At fifty-four, while on a camping trip with her husband, Grace caught her foot in a light cord strung across their tent trailer. Thrown forward, she hit her head with full weight on the bridge of her nose. She hemorrhaged into her spinal cord, and she lost the use of her arms and legs. Very slowly her movements returned, but not completely. Practicing medicine—especially her type of medicine with its house calls and emphasis on obstetrics—became out of the question. At fifty-seven, Dr. Kaiser returned to school, took writing courses, and began a successful new career as a writer.

There may be no such thing as "having it all"—at least, not all of the time. In any case, it doesn't hurt to be fortified in any way one can (something like taking internal vitamins!) by taking action now to prepare for the time when one's role may change.

SOCIETY WON'T HELP VERY MUCH

The first shock of middle age may come when we realize that older people are treated differently. Many women say, "I first realized I was middle-aged when all the young men at cocktail parties looked past me as if I were invisible." It's not fun to be invisible.

Pat Moore, author of *Disguised*, was a twenty-six-year-old reporter and executive in New York when she researched how people react to elders. And she discovered that sometimes they reacted with rudeness and indifference. Dressed and made up to look like an older woman, Pat went into a stationery store to buy a typewriter ribbon. She pretended she couldn't remember the brand name of her typewriter. The salesman impatiently recited the names of the major typewriters, and finally she named one. Pat fumbled as she slowly withdrew money from her purse to pay for her purchase. The salesman was unkind and abrupt.

Pat returned the next day as her twenty-six-year-old self. Again she told the salesman that she had forgotten the name of her typewriter, and again she fumbled while getting the money from her purse. But this time, the salesman was friendly and helpful to this "younger" woman.

Depressing? Yes—if you buy into it. Forewarned is forearmed. When women don't realize how extensive ageism is in our society, they think something is wrong with *them*. Pat Moore said, "The worst part of being treated as if I were not important was that I began to *believe* I was not important."

The present generation of older women is especially vulnerable to this kind of ageism because often they were taught to please other people at the expense of themselves. Women were thought selfish to want something for themselves. "We were brought up to be altruistic—and look where it got us!" Areta Johnson comments dryly.

BREAKING OUT IS HARD TO DO

Sometimes a woman's family can have a vested interest in keeping Mother occupied with their concerns. Husbands are used to having dinner ready at six o'clock. Adult children look for a port in a storm—and a baby-sitter, too. Children may be excited about Mother's 4.0 average at the university; but later they ask, "Why don't you ever bake warm chocolate-chip cookies like Mrs. Scordatto?"

The elderly relatives of the midlifers may present the biggest obstacle of all. They need more attention at the very time their not-so-young daughters are trying for a new life. In our youth-oriented society, we don't quite know what to do with them. The extended family no longer exists. In today's nuclear family, an elderly aunt or grandmother fits into neither the lifestyle nor the prevailing small condominium.

With all these pressures, the "midlifers" are beginning to feel like "lifers," and breaking out of the mold seems to be harder than breaking out of prison! "When is it my turn?" they often wonder.

NEEDED: A BETTER IMAGE

More optimistic views on aging probably are on the way, since society itself is aging. The beauty and warmth of actress Colleen Dewhurst has inspired a young playwright to create a movie script for her. Perhaps soon the media will present more women over fifty as attractive and romantic.

We need a better name than the clinical "postmenopausal." Frances Lear, publisher of Lear's magazine, has found one possibility. You've heard of the YUPPIES, that fast-moving, ambitious group of young adults who drink Perrier and drive BMWs and ate croissants before they became a fast-food item. Says Ms. Lear, "We are the OPALS—Older People with an Active Life Style."

How appropriate! Sand, pressed by the forces of nature, tempered to a dual quality of toughness and crystalline iridescence, becomes an opal, a gem that emits inner fire!

THE GOOD NEWS

If this generation of OPALS has special difficulties, it also has more opportunities for growth than any other generation at any time in history. Many women have taken advantage of those opportunities and reached a happy state of fulfillment. Others, sadly, may believe those opportunities are unattainable.

Life in the late middle years can be not only good, it can be *outstanding!* In her book, *You Can't Count on Dying,* Natalie Cabot reports hundreds of interviews and tests with older adults. She found that when a good adjustment is achieved in midlife, it far surpasses any adjustment reached in earlier years. Those who achieve this degree of self-mastery are the truly successful people of the world. Their sense of well-being does not depend on the changes around them. It depends on the fortress of strength they have built within themselves.

CHAPTER THREE

The Power of Aging

BONUSES AS WE GROW OLDER

Many of the men and women I've met who dread aging seem to overlook the fact that if they work at it, their lives can gain in satisfaction. When people didn't live as long as they do now, they had less time to explore their inclinations, realize their full potential, and reap the benefits that age can bring. Today we are enjoying longer and healthier lives, and we have time and resources that never before have been equaled. Those new resources are available to help us find out who we are and what our purpose is in living.

It helps to know that nature is on our side more than against it. Some positive personality traits develop effortlessly from experience and perspective. In the game of living, at first glance it may look as if youth has all the aces;

but the mature person has integration and authenticity—and those turn out to be trump!

So as you assess your losses, take time also to inventory your new assets, those that are the natural bonuses of growing older.

THE FREEDOM TO CHANGE

With maturity and experience, it is finally easier to throw off the old ideas of how we "ought to be." Years of meeting people with many different values and lifestyles have made their impact. Women by the thousands are looking within, finding their truer selves, and changing their ways of thinking. The old messages that dictate what a woman "should" be doing are still there, but they begin to fade as a new sense of one's individuality emerges at maturity.

It is important to stay open to the idea of change. Life is full of changes. At one time it was right to devote our energies to the job, the children, the large house. But now the children have left home and the house is too large and the career may be on the wane. Is life basically over? Not for those who know they are free to change and grow!

People who resist change become more and more closed to the ever-changing world. Finally they become locked into the old ways, *unable* to change. People who age in this way can become caricatures of their fear. Some will choose anger over happiness, while others retreat in passive submission. Relating to these narrow men and women is unrewarding. They have failed to develop "whole" personalities with a repertoire of behaviors and a variety of responses to the world. These unfortunate people have not learned that to cling to the past is devastating.

ADAPTABILITY

Adaptability is the talent for "going with the flow." And never before has the "flow" been so rapid. Fortunately, the women who now are in late middle age have had to be flexible for most of their lives. As children, they adjusted to the Depression of the 1930s and then to the wartime demands of the 1940s. Their lives became relatively serene during the next decade, but then they had to adjust to the civil unrest of the sixties and the new moral codes and freedoms that followed.

Anita Romero went to work at the telephone company ten years ago so she could pay for her daughter's education at an eastern college. Now Anita must adjust to the knowledge that her daughter is living with a man she met there. Anita worries about her daughter and believes she is making a mistake. But she loves her daughter and she wants to keep communication open, so she adjusts even to this new, unfamiliar lifestyle.

ACCEPTANCE OF DIFFERENCES

Rachel Zane of the Gray Panthers says, "If you know yourself, you can accept differences in other people. You can integrate their ways within your own experience." People who have not learned to know themselves expect other people to be like them. Allowing other people to be themselves is a personal relief as well as a step in the direction of maturity.

At eighty-four, Sarah Lerner believes that when you are older it is easier to accept people the way they are. Sarah is economical with her emotions. She gets upset over major things like bigotry, but she can remain relaxed when a friend becomes overly demanding or difficult. "When you are young, everything is 'do or die,'" says Sarah. "But with age, you learn to be more particular about what you get upset about."

SPONTANEITY

Acceptance and a feeling of freedom can lead to another asset—spontaneity. Many women said they were once shy and fearful about expressing themselves. Now, at fifty or sixty, they feel free to talk to anybody—the garbage collector, the state senator, anybody.

Abraham Maslow wrote that spontaneity is a characteristic of the highly evolved personality. Spontaneous people act in accordance with their natural feelings of the moment. Their actions are not edited by the demands of society or planned in advance. They are open, guileless, and therefore expressive. They do observe the usual conventions of society, realizing that to do otherwise will cause discomfort or embarrassment to others; but they are self-motivated in a unique way, and they are quick to drop conventional behavior when an important issue comes up. Thus, you see many older people demonstrating for world peace.

Rachel Zane says she feels free to look at things "as if I'm seeing them for the first time in my life, without having any preconceived notions. It's almost as if I had a child's point of view again. Once I can see it clearly for what it is, I can adapt to it or change it." This new ability to reevaluate and see things with fresh eyes is the core of creativity.

CREATIVITY

Today many new opportunities exist for men and women to express their perspectives and mental freedom in creative endeavors. Playwriting classes, for example, are filled more with older adults than with eighteen-year-olds. To write a meaningful play, it is necessary first to appreciate and love all kinds of people. After years of identification with Snow White, the older person finally understands that the wicked witch has a "side," too. We've been there. Having experienced all the ages and life situations that led to the present, we have developed compassion.

Kate Maxwell, sixty-five, experienced stress with different role expectations as she went from divorce and financial loss to a new career as a successful actress. Now she tours the country presenting a dramatic play which she wrote about her life. Carol Carson, always an artist, at fifty-eight is beginning to have her work shown in more art galleries, and she is selling more than ever before. Many of the women I talked with are taking notes and plan to devote their later years to writing.

Creative Writing

What can we call a new writer who is fifty, sixty, seventy? An old/new writer? An older writer just beginning? The number of such writers is growing. Sometimes society doesn't know quite what to make of them. The old/new writer has the problem of having few cohorts and even fewer models, being the senior in the writing class, and lacking the encouragement accorded to young writers. What can would-be encouragers say? "You will develop into a fine writer"? (When? Before senility sets in?)

There is an assumption that a late start means you will never get there. Yet many writers who started late achieved greatness. Sondra Zeidenstein accumulated writings and biographies of talented women who got a late start. In her book, *A Wider Giving*, she expresses her delight at reading work by older women. The experiences that were included related to her life in a way that she had not found in other works.

"Times of Silence"

Tillie Olsen, a gifted writer, was in her fifties when her first book was published. In *Silences*, her book on women and creativity, she gives thought to books not written and to the periods in writers' lives when they are not writing. Those are times of "natural silence," times for gestation of ideas and creative renewal. Creative artists require more than talent and desire; they also must have time to create and circumstances that are not opposed to the needs of creativity. There are terrible silences imposed on writers that temporarily block their work. Some examples are illness, the necessity of long working hours, political or religious censorship, a betrayal of creativity through alcohol abuse, or a sacrificing of talent to commercialism.

Women experience still another kind of silence, the silence that prevents a gifted woman from beginning to write. Women are trained to place others' needs first, to enable others to use their talents. Tillie Olsen calls this "foreground silence." A woman may start her creative work later in life when her circumstances improve, or she may never start at all. Virginia Woolf wrote in her diary that if her father were still alive, there would have been no writing, no books.

Women who are raising children have a circumstance that makes sustained creation impossible. Having a child means being constantly interrupted, always available to meet the child's needs. Children need Mother right away, not when the chapter is finished. Women also are more vulnerable to poverty. A male writer may work in a garret, but usually a supportive woman brings him food and sustenance. A woman who runs her own household is forever distracted.

Tillie Olsen suffered a long foreground silence. Twenty years of raising children and working left her too exhausted to write, and her talent seemed to die. When at last she received financial support, it was almost too late. She believed that her most productive years had gone. She felt like an emaciated survivor as she began to write. "I could manage only the feeblest, shallowest growth on that devastated soil," she wrote. But she persevered, and eventually she wrote books that are considered classics. *Tell Me a Riddle* and *Yonnondio: From the Thirties* are well known to students of literature.

Creative Dance

"There is only the dance," said T.S. Eliot.

Life is movement—not just waving your legs and arms about, but the internal movement of every organ of the body. It is not surprising that we can express feelings and discover our own power through movement.

Cora Miller, a slim, energetic woman with smiling eyes and gray hair bound in a ponytail, is a retired professional dancer and teacher. She developed the dance program at Massachusetts State University and taught until she was sixty-seven years old. Now seventy-two, she is a marvelous example of the energizing and creative effect of the dance.

Cora believes that creative dance can enhance our lives at any age. "Everyone has his own dance," she says, "and my job is to facilitate its discovery." Your own dance reflects your age and life experiences.

"Don't be concerned that you might never have studied dance before," Cora says. "Beginners can create with more freshness than advanced students who are more studied in technique."

She recommends that older dancers prepare for her classes with several weeks of stretching exercises, and she helps them to guard their legs, knees, and ankles. She also helps them modify movements that may be difficult for them to perform.

Cora's beliefs are shared by Ruth Pryor, another dancer I talked with. When the first American production of Tchaikovsky's "Swan Lake" opened in Chicago in 1929, ballerina Ruth Pryor was its Swan Queen. Then in her twenties, Ruth was premiere danseuse of the Chicago Civic Opera.

Ruth danced professionally until she was fifty-eight years old. Then she opened the Ballet Theatre School of Dance of Cleveland. As both dancer and teacher, Ruth found that older dancers have energy, enjoy dancing, and bring deeper feeling to their work. They learn steps as well as the younger dancers, but at a slower rate. Ruth, now eighty-two, still has a gemstone inner glow. And she is still dancing!

Dance is a metaphor for dealing with life. It opens up possibilities for powerful, creative response.

Creative Problem Solving

While many people over fifty do begin or renew some kind of specific artistic skill, this is not the total of creativity. A more important area of creativity is in dealing with the problems that life brings. One and one may equal two; but if we rearrange the facts and put them together in a new, imaginative way, the "two" can expand in new directions. A creative approach to life is more important than being able to paint. In fact, those who isolate their creativity in a definite art may not always deal with their personal lives in an enlightened way. See any Hollywood scandal sheet for examples.

A SENSE OF HUMOR

"Laughter is like internal jogging," says Anna Cullinan. "It keeps us well." Fortunately, an increased sense of humor often goes along with an increase in years. Humor depends on perspective, spontaneity, creativity—the assets that seem to be our new treasures.

Many of our famous comediennes are older women. They may have been out of sight for years, "paying their dues" in obscure nightclubs, or perhaps they just now at maturity possess the qualities of perspective that enrich humor. Regardless, we revel in their special talents.

Phyllis Diller lampoons old age in her book, *The Joys of Aging, and How to Avoid Them*. "Sure, there were some brilliant, vital old people," she writes. "Albert Schweitzer was a great humanitarian, but could he get a date for New Year's Eve?" With tongue in cheek, Phyllis "recommends" acting young. "Are you with it?" she asks. "Do you still say words like 'snazzy' and 'my goodness'? Say things like, 'Oh, wow' and 'all righhhhht!' Say 'I can relate to your karma' and 'I've got something heavy to lay on you' even if you don't know what they mean." She asks searching questions, like "Is whip and chill part of your food or sex budget?"

Clare Toth, a psychologist, believes that humor changes your whole being. It is healing, both physically and emotionally. Because it helps people to see themselves and others in a humane way, it brings people together. Perfectionism is a characteristic that doesn't stand up too well under the astute gaze of a humorist. In humor there is an implicit recognition of our human frailties.

INCREASED TOLERANCE FOR STRESS

The ability to handle stress increases with age. "I am no longer rocked by the unexpected," says Rachel Zane.

"The peaks and valleys come closer together, nothing is that serious, nothing is that fantastic, and more of it is good. It all comes together somewhere in the middle."

This relates to Natalie Cabot's findings, reported in her book, *You Can't Count on Dying*. She wrote about the "Rock of Gibraltar" elders who have adjusted to a lifetime of difficulties and yet enjoy life more than ever. They have had practice in dealing with stress over the years, and they have perfected their coping skills as their problems became more formidable. The result is a strengthening of personality.

Many people in this age group have learned to anticipate stressful situations and avoid them, if possible. They also have developed the habit of making lists and providing themselves with other reminders. Most of all, they have learned not to get upset about little things. "Sometimes I get so frustrated when I can't find my glasses," says Catherine James, seventy-three.

" 'Where did I put that?' is such a common stress. But I try to look at it differently. There is nothing wrong with me. I'm not encroaching on Alzheimer's; that's when you forget you have glasses at all. I just have to learn to be more tolerant of myself."

GREATER APPRECIATION OF SMALL THINGS

Still—in a way—nobody sees a flower—really— it is so small—we haven't time—and to see takes time, like to have a friend takes time.
—*Georgia O'Keeffe*

As we grow older, we have the time and perspective to see the abundance of beauty that surrounds us. Barrie Ryan, teacher and journal workshop leader, notes that "young people overlook things. Perhaps they feel they can always go back later to smell the roses. Older people take the time to thank a waitress who delivered their favorite lunch promptly, a friend who wrote a note. They see how precious the most casual of human contact can be."

Barrie urges the men and women in her journal-keeping workshops to recall beauties of nature from their past experiences. "Perhaps they remember a special tree from their childhood. They took the tree for granted when they were ten, but now they realize that the tree was nurturing and important to their growth."

Jane Lancaster, a retired third-grade teacher who has the insight that comes with being seventy, wrote in her journal about the beauty of a tree in her yard. Her young neighbor was irritated that the tree's leaves were always falling over the fence and into his yard. The beauty of the tree enriches Jane's life; and she hopes that in time her neighbor will recognize that although he has the leaves, he also has the same beautiful view that Jane enjoys.

LIBERATION FROM MATERIAL THINGS

Another bonus to growing older is the increased ability to appreciate what one has, and a decreased interest in spending all that time and money shopping. Barrie Ryan notices that this is true for people of all economic circumstances, from people on extremely limited funds to the very wealthy.

Diana Mason, a seventy-five-year-old retired artist in a retirement home in Maryland, comments on material possessions: "When you are young, you want Ethan Allen furniture. When you are older, expensive furniture is seen as something to impress others, and it's of little value to you. It is as though life is saying, 'Enough of that. Now it is time for you.'"

A BOOST FROM BIOLOGY

No more menstrual periods! No more PMS! With childbearing years ending, the hormonal system finally gives us a break. All along, the female and male hormones in our bodies have been doing a balancing act. Now the female hormone, estrogen, decreases. The male hormone decreases too, but it increases in its relative balance with the female hormone. This change in balance is what gives some women whiskers on the chin—but it also releases a surge of energy. If the new energy is harnessed to a meaningful goal, the woman can be newly productive. She becomes more interested in making an imprint on the world. True, it comes at a time when her opportunities may have dwindled. Still, this shift represents a boost in power to help a woman in changing the direction of her life.

Men go the other way, their female hormone outbalancing testosterone, the decreasing male hormone. They become more emotional and nurturing. This can be a difficult time for men, and it comes at an inopportune time for them, too. They are more interested in being close to their children, but the children have moved away and are absorbed with their own lives. They want greater intimacy with their wives, but their wives are off taking courses, working outside the home, resolving community problems. Many men become puzzles to themselves. Carl Jung believed that this change is a common factor in the nervous breakdowns of men in their forties in this country.

In our society, the qualities of competence and self-esteem are more valued than the nurturing qualities. This is not to say that society has the proper values; ideally, a society should reward both traits equally. It is also true that many men are caring and sensitive when young, and many women are dominant and assertive. For the woman who has not had those traits, however, the energies released in the later years are a boon.

THE SURVIVAL ZONE

While it is true that the statistics on heart disease and cancer increase in relation to age range, there is a correction we need to make in those statistics. In the charts, we are competing with twenty-year-old athletes. We have already decided not to judge ourselves by them. There are several aspects of being older that indicate we may hold out for quite a while.

1. *We have survived this far.* The fact that you have lived this long illustrates that your body has something going for it. Whatever its problems, it has proven itself as a viable organism. The first year of life is actually the most precarious. All along the way, younger people with weak hearts, lungs, or livers have succumbed.

   It is good to know that by fifty-five our bodies have proven their ability to survive and that we are not as fragile as we thought. Many late-middle-agers with reasonably healthy bodies who take good care of themselves can endure for a long time.

2. *We are women.* The survival rates in the health charts include that far more precarious organism known as the human male. In the seventy-five- to eighty-year range, there are twice as many women alive as men. (This makes accumulating a series of husbands rather difficult.)

3. *We are in "the survival zone."* A "survival factor" sets in at about fifty-five. Redford B. William, Jr., M.D., and others have conducted extensive studies of heart disease, especially as it relates to Type-A behavior. (The Type-A person, you will remember, is the hard-

driving, compulsive personality.) The folks with biological vulnerability to heart disease usually die or develop the disease at a relatively younger age. Survivors,
even those who are Type-A, seem to be biologically
hardier. In later age, the Type-A person develops a
new hardiness, occasionally even outliving the calmer
Type-B.

This is not to say that we can be content to be Type-A.
There are many reasons to modify Type-A tendencies. For
example, it is hard for the goal-oriented Type-A person to
form close relationships. A fifty- or sixty-year-old person
with no close friends is deprived of an important asset and
source of satisfaction.

So eliminate the high-risk people and those with biological weaknesses—and the statistics are not as bad as they
look. We just need a more relevant chart!

PHYSICAL ASPECTS CAN BE MODIFIED

Most of the physical aspects of aging can be modified. In *Vitality and Aging*, James F. Fries and Lawrence M.
Crapo of the Stanford University School of Medicine wrote,
"Aging and senescence are only loosely related to increasing
chronological age." We all know people of the same age who
differ remarkably in how old they act and look. Many signs
of aging—diminished cardiac reserve, lung capacity, short-
term memory, and social interaction—can be overcome.
There is no limit on our ability to improve our life—at least,
not until very late in life. The vigorous, productive years
can go on almost until the end. Life after fifty is not a
continuous downward slope—or it doesn't have to be.

Here are some aspects of aging and what we can do to
modify them.

Cardiac reserve	Exercise, don't smoke
Osteoporosis	Exercise, increase calcium intake
Physical endurance	Exercise, control weight
Physical strength	Exercise
Pulmonary reserve	Exercise, don't smoke
Reaction time	Increase through training
Skin aging	Use sunscreen creams
Blood pressure	Limit salt, lose weight
Vision	Use glasses
Hearing	Use a hearing aid

It is true, however, that at each succeeding age, more effort is needed. The seventy-year-old who wants to run a long distance must train a lot harder to get into condition than a thirty-year-old runner. Eventually we must decide how much time and effort we want to invest. We can do it all; but—given limited time and other priorities—we may have to make some choices.

SELF-ESTEEM

Sagging skin, brown spots, ten pounds extra around the middle! Despite these inescapable physical facts, many middle-aged and older people still think as well of themselves as they did when they were younger. Growing older is not a reason to develop low self-esteem. Many women find new confidence and self-assurance after fifty. This fact alone speaks of great personal resilience.

SEXUALITY

"The new generation seems to think they discovered sex," complains Mae Rice, a grandmother. "They didn't— we did!"

There is no reason for most older people not to have an active and satisfying sex life as they age. Many women intensify their interest in sex at menopause. Gone is the fear of pregnancy, the inconvenience or side effect of a birth-control pill or device. Writing in *Age Wave*, Ken Dychtwald, Ph.D., reports a recent study of the sexual aspect of life for people aged sixty to ninety. Almost all of them said they still enjoy sexual relations. In *Love, Sex, and Aging*, Edward M. Brecker reports that 80 to 90 percent of married women stay sexually active into their seventies. The figures go down to 50 or 60 percent for single women of that age. Clearly, age is no barrier to the enjoyment of sex.

The image of the older person as sexless needs some rethinking. While bulges and sags do not seem to symbolize sex as well as firm young skin does, perhaps there are more intrinsic qualities that still create the sexual chemistry that brings people together.

Pfeiffer, Verwoerdt, and Davis studied more than five hundred healthy men and women forty-six and older. They recorded some declines in sexual interest and frequency. However, many women in later age groups become widowed or divorced and may not have sexual partners. This may affect the statistics. Pfeiffer and his associates concluded that a continuing sexual capacity is possible for most seniors unless social factors, such as widowhood or the rules of nursing homes, interfere.

Some women who are alone use vibrators to continue the sexual enjoyment they knew before; others resist the idea. For those who are interested in continuing this fundamental pleasure, there are new aids. It is not necessary to haunt an X-rated shop or take a chance on a department-store scalp vibrator. Sex therapists and educators have invented vibrators that are advertised as completely safe and suitable for the purpose. For more information, contact the manufacturers listed in the bibliography at the back of this book.

The most important conclusion to these studies is that people who were sexually active in their middle years have a good chance of continued sexual enjoyment in their later years.

So, we can retain our mental abilities, improve the abilities that have declined through neglect, grow in humor, creativity, and life satisfaction, feel a more intense appreciation of life, and continue to enjoy sex. Not so bad after all!

A GENERATION OF SELF-STARTERS

The presently late-middle-aged generation of women grew up in restricted times, compared to the freedom of today. They lack the feeling of entitlement that young women now possess. Why not become a surgeon? That generation could have thought of many reasons why not. The opportunities they did have came with difficulties and negative injunctions attached. Can anyone over fifty forget the movie, *The Red Shoes*? In that story, a young woman's dedication to the ballet resulted in the destruction of her marriage and death. So much for creative endeavors! Society expected women to be domestic, so any unconventional choices would be very risky. If they wanted to make something unusual happen, they would have to arrange it themselves, with little or no outside encouragement.

This generation is geared to self-determination. As students, they need no deadline or exam; they are learning because they wish to learn. As employees, they work without the need of supervision. This ability comes in handy after fifty. Many men and women who did not obtain their higher degrees are self-educated through extensive reading.

Because they learned willingly and are able to accept new situations, they are good teachers for others.

GOOD SOCIAL SKILLS

Adapting to change, raising children, and dealing with the community has strengthened women's natural ability to persuade, relate, and deal with differences in others. Many women are the peacemakers of a community. They are empathetic listeners and good mediators for those who are in conflict.

Another asset that women have going for them is that they know how to find and utilize support from other women. And they know how to give support in return. All of the successful and happy women I talked with emphasized the importance of communicating on a regular basis with other vital, positive women.

IMPORTANT CONNECTIONS

Women over fifty are likely to have grown children who are also a permanent kind of support group. Many women experience stress in relating to their adult children; but thanks to the ability of this generation to communicate so well, they also find some mutuality with their children. They believe their children are genuinely interested in their happiness and welfare.

The steadfastness of this generation of husbands and wives becomes an important asset as they age. In this impersonal world, with everyone bent on their "own thing," the supportive role seems to be disdained. In a long marriage, the husband and wife fall into this role without feeling sacrificed.

George Gafner, a social worker, counsels veterans of World War II and their families. He is impressed with the strength of commitment these couples have. The husbands and wives are each other's support during the illnesses and crises of aging.

Stability

Young people today have many choices in career, in love, in family planning. One choice they do not always have is stability. Relationships are transient, with society becoming more mobile than ever. The woman over fifty is more apt to have a basic structure to her life. She may make drastic changes in her life—a divorce, a new career; but there's a comforting sameness to it, too. She can be reached by mail; her address usually doesn't shift every year. There is (or was) a husband who stood by her for many years. She's a good bet for not having AIDS or a lot of bounced checks. She can be a blood donor because she is not apt to be on drugs. She already knows what kind of fashion she likes and people she enjoys, so she can relax about it and not complicate her life with decisions. If the going is rough in your relationship with her, you can be sure she will not abandon you but will stay in there and work to improve the situation. In that way, she offers stability to her children and to the world.

"Home, Sweet Home"

The cost of houses has escalated to a point that young couples cannot afford homes and wonder if they ever will. A forty-year-old English professor who has distinguished himself at his university told me that he and his family cannot buy a home. Financial institutions have created new kinds of mortgages that often lock young buyers into a lifetime commitment to earn two incomes. But the older generation of women is more likely to have a place to call home, and often a home that is comfortable and attractive.

OPTIMISM

"We grew up with a bright view of the world," says Helen Briggs, a social worker. "There were difficulties, true; but we believed everything would be all right." Today's young people grew up in the shadow of nuclear war. War is no longer a case of men going off to fight in the front; it is potentially a case of destroying the race. We were able to maintain a "tomorrow will be better" outlook. We also grew up in a much safer world, without the fear of crime and violence that mar a young child's life today. We could explore the neighborhood without fear. We attended college without being troubled about the new finding that one of every six female students will be raped on campus. Our dormitory rooms needed no keys; the main theft was cookies from home stolen by hungry friends. We may have lived in a fool's paradise, with not as safe a world as we thought, but we had a feeling of safety and security.

How fortunate it is that the characteristics of this generation of late-middle-aged women—flexibility, adaptability, compassion, self-motivation—turn out to be the very traits that lead to successful later years for anyone. Today's women have lived through drastic social changes and values. Each change has forced them to reevaluate themselves and their lives. In contrast, men are encouraged to act, to push forward toward their goals with relatively little introspection. To the extent this is true, women are much better equipped to age with satisfaction.

INTEGRATION AND INSIGHT

In *Modern Man in Search of a Soul*, Carl Jung writes about an increase in a person's ability to integrate life experiences—past, present, inner, and outer—to form new meaning, which can be called "insight." He says that while it is "almost a sin—and certainly a danger—for a young person to be too much occupied with himself, for the aging person it is a duty and a necessity to give serious attention to himself." Jung recommends life review and reflection. Through the process, we can gain fresh insights that enable us to reap the rewards offered in the second half of life.

The most profound insights may have been found by people in their seventies and eighties. Pearl Buck said, at seventy-nine, "I am a far more valuable person today than I was fifty years ago, or forty years, twenty, or even ten. I have learned so much since I was seventy! I can honestly say that I have learned more in the last ten years than in any previous decade. This, I suppose, is because I have perfected my techniques so that I no longer waste time in learning to do what I have to do. Year by year we work for techniques in order to master ourselves and reach a growing understanding of ourselves and others. Happiness is based upon this primary understanding."

In her book *At Seventy: A Journal*, May Sarton writes, "I realize that seventy must seem extremely old to my young friends, but I actually feel much younger than I did when I wrote *The House by the Sea* six years ago. . . . And that, as far as I can see, is because I live more completely in the moment these days, am not as anxious about the future, and am far more detached from the areas of pain, the loss of love, the struggle to get the work completed, the fear of death."

Detachment from areas of pain does not mean detachment from the pleasures of life. In fact, the opposite is more apt to be true. Older people have an increased sensitivity and appreciation of the good things. May Sarton talks about the miracle of daffodils, robins and goldfinches, music, friendships, just being alive.

ACQUIRING THE POWER

How can one acquire all of these qualities that lead to successful living?

Although most come naturally with age, they do need encouragement and development. They are most apt to come to the person who has embarked on an inward journey. We will talk about that inward journey in another chapter.

CHAPTER FOUR

Surviving in a Difficult World

SOME WOMEN WHO MADE IT,
AND SOME OTHERS WHO DIDN'T

Many of the women I've met and talked with had plenty of reason to give up. Raised to consider other people's needs first, given little encouragement to develop themselves, now facing the physical problems and the social problems of being an "older woman," often they floundered. But a certain tenacity, a thumbs-up to the society that brought them to this place, and a determination to survive, gave them a strength they didn't know they had. When the difficulties of life started to pile up, each woman had a time when she felt her back was "against the wall," and each one recalls a moment when she decided to break free.

Once they had made the decision to survive, these women looked around and found others to give them a boost. The pressures of their families had kept them in a rut. Now they needed allies somewhere out there in the world. The kind of help varied. Some found it in support groups, psychotherapy, classes, workshops, spiritual teachers, books. But no one tried to do it alone.

"There are limits to individual coping," writes Leonard I. Pearlin, Ph.D., a leading research psychologist studying stress at the Developmental Institute of the University of San Francisco. The multiple losses faced by the older person can result in a level of stress that is, at least temporarily, beyond the ability to handle alone. Men and women who have failed to cope with a lot of stresses at once should not feel it is all "their fault." At the same time, they can work on their own coping skills.

If you have lost your husband, your home, your youth and beauty, your health, your car, lowered your income due to retirement, and moved away from your established community, you are building your stress points right off the chart! Don't be surprised or feel inadequate if you don't bounce back right away, particularly if you are without outside help.

After decades of socially defined roles, it can be bewildering to have those roles fading. Does a twenty-eight-year-old son really need his mother to do his laundry? Probably not; and it's time for both mother and son to break with the past. The break can be viewed as a loss; yet, strangely, that very loss may liberate the woman to find some new dimension in herself.

The new goals chosen by the women who are happy generally lie in one of four different directions: new involvement with careers or community; creativity; activism; or spirituality. Many of these women already have had more than one goal in their lives, and they are not at all taken back by the discovery that it's time for a new one.

CAROLINE: A NEW CAREER

"We were the last generation to believe that the only role for women was to get married, have children, and live happily ever after," declares Caroline Anderson, a dynamic sixty-year-old writer living in the Northwest. "It was the 'happily ever after' that didn't always come," she adds ruefully.

As a young woman, Caroline did all the things that were expected. In the early 1950s, society was demanding more and more scientists, so Caroline studied chemistry at a top university. There she met Jim, who seemed to be Prince Charming himself—tall, handsome, working toward his Ph.D. in another of the sciences, biology. Jim was a bit quiet, but there was a reassuring saying about withdrawn men: "Still waters run deep." Shortly after they were married, Caroline would find that the waters could become troubled and she was in deeper than she realized.

Caroline got her degree; but women of the fifties were expected to give up or postpone any career intentions and devote themselves to their roles of wife and mother. So Caroline stayed home and had four children. (If this was your career, why not do it on a grand scale?)

The "still waters" became turbulent. If Jim was going to support a wife, he wanted all the services thereof. He became obsessively concerned about his masculine image, and he was afraid the children were usurping his place with Caroline. He began to drink more and more, and his demands increased. "I want my eggs fried sunny-side-up—not scrambled, not flopped over, sunny-side-up. . . . Why didn't you iron my pajamas? . . . While you're up, how about bringing me a martini?" Jim's drinking soon progressed to complete dependence on alcohol.

Caroline raised the children, took care of the house and

checkbook, drove the car after Jim's license was taken away on a DWI charge; in short, she took on the total responsibility for their lives.

Caroline stuck with this unsatisfying marriage for twenty-one years. A young woman of the nineties might wonder why she did it. In those days it was evident: "You don't give up on somebody who is ill. . . . Marriage is for life."

Eventually Jim was hospitalized for two months, and Caroline was forced to examine her life. She faced the fact that she could no longer endure living this way, and she filed for divorce.

Caroline was forty-two years old. She didn't know how she would provide for herself and her four children. What could she do? Years of making peanut butter sandwiches hadn't sharpened her skills in chemistry. "I might be allowed to wash the test tubes," she thought wryly.

Not only was Caroline lacking any current career skills; she also lacked self-confidence. A new personality *and* a new career were in order.

She began by taking a psychological aptitude test. The results indicated that she had some aptitude to be a writer. Caroline returned to the university, studied writing, and began to sell a few articles to the local newspaper.

To succeed in her new career, Caroline needed to overcome her lack of self-esteem and learn to be assertive. She also had to confront her anger toward Jim. Caroline entered a psychotherapy group to achieve both of these objectives. There she was able to express her anger about the past. After many months, she was able to let go of the resentment and get on with her life.

After the divorce, Caroline moved to the Northwest for a fresh start. At first, thinking that men were listened to more than women, she signed her columns with her initials instead of her first name so readers would think she was a man. In time, more newspaper publishers picked up her column, and she was treated for the first time as a professional writer. Her career took off, and she became financially successful as a journalist. She hosted popular radio and television shows, where she was known for her keen wit.

But Caroline's most agonizing life crisis was yet to come. At fifty, she developed a serious liver disorder that left her bloated with abdominal cysts. Her heart was strained by the liver problem, and her lifestyle was restricted. "I felt so grotesque. At times I didn't want to go out of the house so people could see me. I had to go to my job, though, and that was fortunate." Her doctors told her she had liver cancer and hadn't long to live. For months she struggled under that death sentence.

Then the cancer diagnosis was proven wrong. But the cysts remained. Surgery was hazardous, and the survival rate was discouraging. But Caroline's doctors told her she would be bedridden if she didn't have the operation. Knowing she would be unsatisfied with any life but a productive one, Caroline scheduled the surgery. She survived the illness, and now she has new energy and health. She walks two miles every day and is writing a book about her life.

How does she feel about the past? She takes satisfaction in recalling that she had a home and family as well as a career, even though she didn't have them at the same time. Caroline says, "We are the first generation of women to have it all—but we had to work like hell for it!"

Caroline found that success in the professional world required her to become verbally assertive, especially when she was supervising the work of others. Sometimes, in the middle of a forceful statement, her mind flashes back to the shy woman she used to be. "I'm still haunted by that submissive woman," Caroline says.

What Can We Learn from Caroline?

Caroline's story illustrates many of the obstacles placed in the path of women of this generation: outdated career skills, strong societal messages, an unenlightened husband. Her story points out qualities and strategies that enable women to find new meaning in their lives.

1. *Self-affirmation:* "I am me."
2. A certain *independence* from what society says she should do.
3. *Determination.* (Caroline calls herself "stubborn.") She spent twenty-one years in her no-win situation; but with her back against the wall, she came through.
4. *Personality change.* Caroline knew that her lack of self-esteem was holding her back from the life she wanted, and she worked hard to become more confident and outgoing.
5. *"Letting go."* Facing her anger with her husband and dealing with it in group therapy helped her to release the past and free her energies for the important present.
6. *Courage* to face serious illness and death. Perhaps years of self-definition and confidence had prepared her for this awesome challenge.
7. *Humor,* a talent that often develops with age, enabled her to look at life with further perspective.
8. *Faith* in herself. "I don't let myself down," she says. To meet dynamic Caroline is to know the truth of those words.

KATE: A CREATIVE WOMAN COMES OF AGE

At age sixty-five, Kate Maxwell has a quiet charm. Her blonde hair waves casually about a face that has held its unusual beauty. Kate grew up in southern Texas, the third child of a charming, charismatic minister and his dutiful wife who was constantly aware that the parishioners' eyes were watching. Her father was devoted to working long hours. When he had a few days off, he'd hold a tent revival meeting in one of the surrounding towns that had no preacher.

The Depression hit their little community hard. Kate's family had never had enough money, but then the unemployed and the hungry began to show up at their door. Soon the churchyard became a campground for needy people. Kate's mother baked meatloaf every morning, and Kate helped her serve it to the homeless people on the parsonage lawn. She learned to feel comfortable with people of any ethnic or economic background. "That experience enriched my life," Kate claims.

Kate admired her father, as did the members of the congregation. Some of the female members of his flock apparently became too fond of him, and he became romantically involved with one of them. He was then promptly dismissed as pastor of that church, and he left town in disgrace. "I didn't see him again until just recently," relates Kate.

Kate inherited the responsibilities of the family—a chronically unhappy mother who was always "having the vapors," a mentally handicapped older sister, a pampered younger sister. Her brother was away at the university, so Kate became head of the household. Kate felt needed but not valued. She felt that she was the strong one, the conscientious worker who took seriously the high ethical values of her religious upbringing.

She had expected to go on to college, but when she was sixteen her mother told her she would have to settle for a typing course. Her mother saw to it that her brother was able to continue his education, though. "After all," her mother said, "someday he will be the head of a family." Kate didn't get her bachelor's degree until she was fifty years old.

Kate reflects, "Younger women don't realize how things used to be. They never had to fight for the things they have been given. They can be lawyers or surgeons. They accept those things as their birthright. For a woman of my generation, those opportunities were usually not possible."

Kate had always been fascinated by the theatre. She had a beautiful singing voice, and in 1943 she left home to join the U.S.O. as an entertainer. Her confidence grew as she made business arrangements for the overseas tours, acted and sang for the troops, and won acclaim from audiences all over the world.

On tour in Tokyo, she met Charlie, a handsome enlisted man. Charlie saw her show and went backstage to meet her. She was not permitted to date enlisted men, and so she declined his invitation to have dinner with him. But when he called her again and again, she was unable to resist going out with this magnetic man. She soon found herself madly in love and planning a wedding.

When Kate married Charlie, she thought her life was going to be happy ever after. Charlie had graduated from an Ivy League college. He was brilliant, witty, handsome— and broke. Kate paid for the wedding and their new Buick convertible. She supported them while Charlie went back to school, this time to study cinematography. Eventually he began to produce and direct films.

Marriage nearly ruined Kate. Charlie was so charming, so knowledgeable! People clustered around him, while Kate became a nonentity in his shadow. Charlie began spending more and more time with his friends from the studio. Their conversations centered around the business of making movies, and Kate was simply left out. Always in the back of her mind was the realization that while Charlie had two degrees, she had never been to college. After their fourth child was born, Kate gained weight as she became more and more submerged. Eventually she just gave up trying to please Charlie.

When Kate turned forty, Charlie delivered the final insult that ended their marriage. He revealed that he had been repeatedly unfaithful to her, and then he left her for a woman who was twenty-three—the age Kate had been when they met. Kate, who had never felt loved as a child, had poured all her love into the marriage. She was devastated. Her self-confidence was at low ebb and she wondered what she could do with the rest of her life.

Charlie sent money for child support, but not enough for Kate and the children to have a good life. Money went farther in Mexico. She moved to Guadalajara, where for $5 a week she hired a young woman to help her with the children. Then she went to work on her physical well-being. She jogged, she swam, she learned yoga and tennis. The excess weight dropped off and she regained her self-confidence. Friendships with both men and women nourished her emotional need for support.

Kate took time to explore her abilities, and she discovered she had a talent for writing. Soon she was selling articles about Mexican culture. She returned to the theatre, and again she became sought after as an actress. Kate felt her world turn around. She realized that people found her interesting and attractive, and she no longer felt stupid or unimportant.

When her mother had a heart attack, Kate returned to Texas and stayed with her in the hospital until she died. After the funeral, Kate tried to contact Charlie, only to find that he had filed suit for desertion and had sold her home in California. When she tried to compete for jobs, she had very little success. She was forty-eight years old and, although she still retained a glamorous appearance, younger actresses got the jobs. She realized that her best chance for survival would be in getting an education. Kate applied for financial aid and enrolled in college.

When her youngest child left home to live with his now wealthy father, Kate was alone. She had no savings, no support from anyone, either financial or emotional. Her sons preferred to be with Charlie, who told them she was inferior. Her brother and sisters criticized her divorce, which was considered immoral by their church. Her mother was dead and she didn't know if her father was still living. She thought about returning to Mexico, but she wanted somehow to be reconnected with her children.

Her despair reached a peak. It seemed no one really loved her or even cared what happened to her. She thought so little of herself that she began to question the value of living. Her thoughts turned to her father, who believed in forging ahead in spite of all obstacles. She had tried, but maybe there is a limit to trying.

Then one morning she decided she had had enough of misery and defeat. She got some butcher paper, wrote a message to herself, and taped it around the room. The message written in large capital letters was: IF YOU'RE GOING TO LIVE—LIVE, DAMN IT! LIVE IT FULLY!

"I made up my mind that I *was* going to live, that I *was* strong," Kate told me. The decision required her again to turn herself around, find her self-confidence, and explore her talents once more.

Stretch Yourself!

Kate had learned her father's credo: "Stretch yourself as far as you can, and do as much as you can." She rediscovered that she could present herself well and that she could make a living as a writer and editor. Again she returned to the university, and when she was sixty years old, she received a master's degree in drama.

Kate told me that the years between sixty and sixty-five have been the most productive of her life. She is creative, resourceful about finding writing jobs, talented, and admired. She has written plays and acted in local productions. Recently she wrote a musical comedy about the stages of her life in this unique generation. She plays herself, and has taken the show around the country. She is able to market herself well, and she has a new, positive, hard-won concept of herself. She is proud that she could manage another remarkable change in her personality.

Kate saw her father when he was eighty-eight years old, just before he died. He was still charming, optimistic, and had a sparkling humor. Kate was glad to be reconciled with her past. After all, she had learned her survival skills from her father.

Kate will reach out and be interested in life for as long as she lives—and that could be a very long time.

ANNA: ON THE FOREFRONT OF CHANGE

Anna Cullinan has made it a personal mission to find out why men have more power in our culture than women. She recognized years ago that she would need to incorporate some of that power personally, if she was going to make the changes she saw as necessary in our society.

At fifty-seven, Anna is exuberant and compelling. She smiles with warmth and confidence, and her full, throaty voice is punctuated often with laughter that seems to affirm life. Her eyes light up, and you feel you have known her for years.

She is a dynamic composite of many cultures. Her father was Choctaw Indian and German, her mother Mexican and Irish. She was told that "children should be seen and not heard," and Anna tried to comply.

Anna grew up poor, first in a copper-mining town in Arizona and later in a coal-mining town in Wyoming. Even today she remembers the sound of the mine whistle signaling the injury or death of so many miners.

Anna had two assets: her sharp intelligence, which was recognized early by teachers, and her lively interest in life. Always observant, she learned a few important life lessons from her childhood. She saw her mother as a powerful woman but frustrated, because she had not been permitted to go beyond ninth grade. From that, Anna understood the need for women to be more independent, and she grasped the importance that education would have in that. She learned to feel good about herself through the influence of her strong and supportive parents. Paradoxically, however, she also picked up the idea that a woman's contribution was not as valued as a man's. At mealtime, she saw that the men were served first, children next, and women had the cooled-off leftovers.

In general, the women in Anna's family were women who *did* things. At an early age, Anna knew how to pick carrots and potatoes, milk cows, grow plants. These basic skills gave her a feeling of achievement. "If you learn survival skills," her parents told her, "you become strong. You will never be poor." Later, Anna taught those survival skills to her children. "Working with your hands," she told them, "will make you feel good about yourself. It's better than watching TV."

As a young typist at an adoption agency in Phoenix, Anna worked for a woman who effected an important change in her life. Helen was a Sioux Indian, strong, independent, regal, tall—everything Anna wanted to be. At the same time, Helen had a special warmth that attracted people to her.

Anna saved $176, and she wanted to travel. But she had

no luggage. Having precious little experience with shopping, Anna asked Helen to go to a department store with her and help her to select the right luggage. Helen picked out two matching cases that cost $200. "These will last a long time," she told Anna. But Anna had only $176, and she couldn't buy the set. "I'll have to save some more money and come back later," she told the sales clerk.

"What are you going to put in these suitcases?" Helen inquired on the way home.

"Nothing, I guess. I don't have enough money to buy any new clothes to put in them."

"Where are you going to take the suitcases?"

"I don't have any money now, so I guess nowhere," Anna shrugged. "Why are you asking me these questions?"

"I want you to think," Helen answered. "How is having expensive suitcases going to help you in life?"

Anna realized they were not going to help.

"Why don't you go to college?" Helen asked.

"I can't afford it."

"Instead of buying suitcases, let's look at college tomorrow."

Helen took her to Phoenix Junior College, where the tuition was $45 a semester. Anna enrolled immediately. Later she won a scholarship and was able to continue her education at Arizona State University. There, still another mentor encouraged Anna, seeing something in her that she did not yet see in herself. He helped her to apply for graduate study in social work at UCLA. After a year she returned to Arizona and began working in child welfare on the Navajo reservation at Flagstaff.

Anna married at twenty-eight. Her marriage was a long, loving relationship that lasted for twenty-one years, until her husband died in 1982. They had four children. As foster parents, they also cared for thirty other children—street kids, some of them disturbed. "But sometimes the worst of the troublemakers turned out to be the winners," she told me proudly.

It was during her marriage that Anna began to think about politics as a new career. She was distressed at the inadequate funding that the state government gave to education of children. Anna decided that being a mother wasn't enough. The way to do the most for *all* children was to be involved with the legislature.

Anna felt good about herself as a person; but her early conditioning had taught her to be submissive. Now she needed to affirm the part of herself that was assertive. She talked with her father. "You told me, 'Children should be seen and not heard,'" she said. "Now they say older people should be quiet. When do I get to speak?" Anna decided the time was now.

The Secrets of Anna's Power

Anna realized that if she was to achieve what she wanted, she would need to find a way to have more influence in the world.

"What do men do that enables them to exert power?" she wondered.

Her brother had a business with forty people working under his direction. What did he know that she didn't know? She observed that instead of remaining focused on the details of the business, he looked at it in a broader perspective. He also used proven techniques of relating to people and influencing them. Anna believes these qualities are essential to anyone who wants to advance.

Anna attended a seminar on personality types, where she gained insight into the kinds of personality growth she was seeking. She learned that women tend to be highly detailed. Many vocations—accounting and homemaking, for example—reward this trait. But in order to "move up" it is necessary to branch out from a focus on detail to a broader focus. Women need to be more dominant, taking charge and influencing others rather than pleasing them. Men are able to make the leap more easily because they are given more opportunities to be in charge. Anna believes that women can use their skill at attention to details and combine it with a broader view and more aggressive management style. Thus they can be more effective in positions of power.

She found organizations that teach the skills she needed. One is Toastmasters International, an organization of people who meet regularly to practice public speaking techniques. In cities and towns across the nation, its members meet over a meal. They learn how to become better organized and how to present their thoughts—the very techniques of power. And they learn how to use humor to their advantage. Humor, Anna believes, enables a person to enjoy life, branch out, and make needed connections with others. "Humor is not just telling a joke," she explains. "It's a new way of perceiving life and expressing it with amusement."

For more information on Toastmasters International, contact your local organization listed in the telephone directory; or write to Toastmasters International, P.O. Box 10400, Santa Ana, California 92711.

Anna found another group that teaches important life skills: the Dale Carnegie organization, also spread across the nation. Its fourteen-week course teaches specific leadership skills. There is a fee for the course. However, the books that contain Dale Carnegie's basic principles are available at bookshops and public libraries. His famous book, *How to Win Friends and Influence People,* has been a bestseller for many years. Other books by Dale Carnegie are listed in the bibliography.

Another step Anna took was to set a goal. As a social worker she had seen so many defeated women who had let life "just happen," and she vowed not to make that mistake in her life. She was determined to work toward achieving her goal—the state legislature.

As a young girl she had learned from her mentors, and now she looked again for role models—women who had made it in politics. She found the models she wanted, and she organized the Executive Women's Council of Southern Arizona to meet other women who are powerful and knowledgeable. Anna surrounded herself with people who have a positive outlook on life.

Anna won her political campaign and was elected as a representative to the Arizona legislature in 1975 and 1976. While she was attending sessions in Phoenix, her husband stayed home with the children. "She did it for me while I was in Vietnam," he said. "Now I can do the same for her."

Anna was forty-nine when her husband died. She found she could not deal with the loss alone, and typically she helped to organize W.O.W., a support group of men and women who have lost a spouse.

Anna developed bone cancer soon after the death of her husband. The illness limited her strength, and she was expected to die; but eight years later, she is still active.

"Is cancer the toughest thing a person can face?" I asked her.

"No," said Anna. "It's the low value our society places on women. I was told once that if a man had to pay for all the jobs his wife does, it would cost him a hefty sum. If she's worth it, give it to her!"

Anna told me about a man who sat next to her at a political meeting. He introduced himself. "I'm Judge Fremont." Anna said, "I am Representative Anna Cullinan." "What company do you represent?" he asked. "No, I'm a state representative," Anna answered. "Well, what do you sell?" "Nothing," replied Anna. "Judge, I make the laws that you enforce."

ELSIE: A TRIUMPH OF THE SPIRIT

I met Elsie Western when she was seventy. She was a slim woman dressed in a pink jumpsuit. Her voice was soft, and her eyes were lit with the glow that comes with spiritual growth. She was living in a small trailer in Tucson. Shelves of old books made up most of her few possessions. She was ill with cancer, yet still was enjoying her friends and following her life goal.

Elsie did not come easily to that goal. Her early life made growth difficult. She grew up in a small town near Duluth, Minnesota. It was a beautiful place on Lake Superior, but cold and remote. Her parents were Finnish immigrants, hard-working people who seldom had time to talk, and Elsie was their only child. Her mother had three cows to milk and feed, and her father had a horse. Elsie learned early in life to work with her hands.

Elsie's world was one block long—the tiny Finnish settlement in town, where no one spoke English. In fact, no one spoke much to her at all. Elsie's mother and the other women kept to themselves. The Finnish people were looked down on by the rest of the community, and school was difficult for Elsie because she knew no English. Elsie felt alone.

When she graduated from high school in 1934, she was still shy and alone. She felt she had nothing going for her. She hadn't done all that well in school, she had no special talents, she wasn't pretty, and she had no social or other skills that would help her to succeed in the world. Elsie felt that the future offered little or nothing for her, a girl with no assets. She felt too shy to go to college, and she saw marriage as a trap that would keep her in her small world.

She saved enough money to take a bus to New York City, where she got a job as a housekeeper. This was her first contact with the outside world, and it opened her eyes.

She watched the affluent, successful family she worked for, and she learned how one could talk and act in new ways. Still, she felt ill at ease in the city, and she returned to Minnesota.

Elsie realized by now that what she wanted to do was to learn—not the kind of learning that she would find in college, but learning about the meaning of life itself and her connection with God.

To Elsie's surprise, she succeeded in getting a job as a receptionist in the admitting office of a large hospital. At the same time, she came across a few books written by spiritual leaders of that time, Dr. Glen Clark and Dr. Frank Lebach. She was delighted to find that there are great people in the world who are not Lutheran or Presbyterian!

Elsie discovered that her mission in life was to educate not only herself but others in the spiritual possibilities of their lives. She had no speaking ability, no powers of persuasion, but she had found her tools. "Books are my tools," Elsie said. She began to build up a small collection of books on spiritual growth, and she lent them to doctors in the hospital, to ministers, and to others she met. Several of the ministers were so impressed that they branched out into metaphysical study themselves, and some went into the field of spiritual healing.

Elsie felt herself expanding. She went to workshops given by Dr. Lao Russell and other spiritual leaders. She gradually developed a talent for friendship. Her mission gave her the ability to rise above her shyness. She talked with people and linked them up not only with books and spiritual leaders but with each other.

Elsie had hundreds of friends in Tucson. One of them, Helen Briggs, told me she met Elsie at a meeting of the Women's International League for Peace and Freedom. Elsie discovered they had many mutual interests and she got Helen in touch with others. Elsie subscribed to a number of newsletters that gave information on national concerns. She had articles reproduced, and she gave them away. Her quiet influence seemed to spread in all directions. She didn't know anything about "power talk," but she had a large circle of devoted friends.

Elsie's Beliefs

Elsie experienced deep happiness by following her spiritual path. "This is what the world needs," she believed. "The earth plane is a school where we learn the lessons we need for life on a higher plane." She believed that the world is on the wrong path, following false values. "Civilization may be at a critical point, and spiritual people need to work hard. Many of the choices now being made are negative. The phenomenon of Elvis, for instance, contributes to the worship of fame and money. Instead of putting our energy and support into such nonsense, we need to help the world and increase true understanding. Women should ask themselves not whether Elvis is alive, but important questions: Why were they born? What is the purpose of living?"

Elsie did not fear death. "I have done what I could with my life. I have learned, and I have made a good start for a new life" (in the spiritual dimension). When Elsie died, I wrote: Now we can rest in assurance that Elsie has once more broken through limitations—those of this world. Her growth and knowledge will again be expanded by her Creator.

JANET: CLOUDS IN PARADISE

Janet Smithson had a perfect life, she thought. She was surrounded by good friends from her bridge club in Omaha. "The girls" had played bridge every week for thirty years—through weddings, babies, affairs, the children leaving home, hair turning gray—everything. When Janet's husband, Henry, died, her friends were there to comfort her with sympathy and support.

One day at the bridge table, Janet remarked, "Nebraska's snowstorms sometimes make me feel so *isolated.*" The group discussed this mutual source of distress, and they decided to move en masse to Florida. Within a year the group had relocated in Sarasota, where life and the weekly bridge games continued as usual, even though they were older and had become sensitive to the cold.

Janet was content, there in the Land of Sunshine. Oh, she missed Henry, of course; but she had her friends. She even had an ace up her sleeve—her talent in oil painting, a serious hobby that she continued to enjoy in the new tropical surroundings.

But Janet overlooked one thing. She had always depended so completely on the group that she'd felt no need or desire to explore her options in either her old hometown or her new surroundings in Florida. Now, with Henry gone, she felt especially uneasy about trying new things—churches, book clubs, the neighbors. Suddenly, she felt embarrassed about the sagging of her chin, and the sparkle in her eyes seemed to have vanished. She was afraid that strangers would see only an old woman—not that special person she felt she was. The neighbors who were her age looked—well, *old*, and they seemed to be rather dull. The younger neighbors had noisy parties and they drank too much. Janet withdrew from any association with them. Their children, the teenagers on the block, were an especially aggravating group. "How can parents let their young people walk down the streets wearing such odd clothes and strange hairdos?" Janet wondered. "I'll just bet they're on their way to pick up drugs!"

Janet prided herself on being part of the sensible, compatible bridge group from Omaha. But gradually, the members of the group began to leave for extended periods to travel or visit their children. Then one by one these old friends became ill, and some died. It was getting harder and harder to get a foursome together to play bridge.

Janet remembered her other hobby—the ace up her sleeve. "Now is the time to be creative," she declared. And she set up her easel in the yard, and she began to paint.

One afternoon, Janet wondered why she could barely see the brush strokes she had painted a few days before. Perhaps she had not used enough paint. She spread more on her palette. That didn't look right, either. Janet realized with a shock that she was losing her eyesight.

Janet was alone. She had lost her creative outlet and her friends, too. Sadly, her life began to revolve around ill health. Soon her only social contacts were her frequent visits to the doctor.

Janet's Dilemma

Janet had prepared for her older years in every way but one, and that turned out to be the critical area. In her early-middle years, she made no effort to branch outside her comfortable life and familiar friends. She kept the status quo.

With her eye on the calendar of her life, she might have realized she needed to expand her interests. She liked to paint; she could have joined a painting class or a group of artists or the docent group at an art museum. Painting is an expression of the inner self; but this interest, as with any interest, could have been used to enlarge her circle of acquaintances. Those acquaintances may or may not have become friends, but they might have served an important function. Through them, Janet might have learned to communicate with people of different ages and various interests. She could have developed some group skills that later would have made a difference in her ability to replace the old friends.

Janet stuck to people her own age, thus limiting her social experience. Younger people provide stimulation, a refreshing change, partly because they tend to be spontaneous and role-free. And friends who are older can share the benefits of their life experiences. By their example, our older friends can alleviate many of our fears and help pull us through to another decade.

BARBARA: THE PERILS OF A PERFECT MARRIAGE

Barbara Watson is another woman who "had it all"—a lovely home in Milwaukee, another lakeside vacation home, four children, a community filled with friends. Best of all, she had Sam—handsome, sensitive, loving Sam, a financially successful insurance agent. Barbara also had a career as a teacher in the local school system. She was friendly and sociable, and she and Sam entertained frequently. They loved to dance, and organized a group that met regularly for dinner and dancing at the country club. The women lined up to dance with Sam.

As Barbara grew into middle age, Sam continued to tell her how beautiful she was. "He was so good for my morale," Barbara told me. For forty years, Sam drove her to work when the roads were icy. He scraped the snow off her windshield, he carried the groceries into the house for her every Saturday. He took care of all their needs.

For years they had spent the month of August at their lakeside home. Before starting the five-hour drive, Sam kept a routine appointment with his doctor. His blood pressure was up a little, but the doctor told him to enjoy his vacation. "The rest will be good for you," he said.

When they arrived at the lake home, Sam carried the bags upstairs. When he didn't return after a few minutes, Barbara rushed to their bedroom. She found him collapsed on the bed, dead at the age of sixty.

After the funeral, their friends of thirty and forty years came to call and invited her to dinner. But then they faded away. First, they dropped her from the dance club. She tried to keep the friendships alive; but entertaining—with silver and crystal and four-course dinners in the custom of the community—was too difficult to handle alone. There were no support groups in her small town, and after a while her friends told her it was time for her to "get over Sam's death." Barbara says now that she may have detected a little satisfaction in her friends. For many years they had envied her for having her perfect husband, Sam. Now they seemed almost glad that she was in this predicament! When she complained, they implied that she had been spoiled. Lacking the emotional support she needed, Barbara sold her homes in Wisconsin and moved to California to be closer to her daughter and the grandchildren.

As an insurance agent, Sam had written lists of advice to his clients on what wives needed to know in case their husbands died. But he had never given a copy of the list to Barbara. She found the list among his papers. A client who called to express her sympathy said, "Now who will help me with all my problems?" Barbara thought, "And who will help *me*?" Sam had taken care of the car, the appliances, and the bills.

Barbara's trouble started when the sewer backed up on the day of the funeral. Repairmen were hired to fix it. Barbara returned to her home to find her patio in shambles. Concrete blocks were broken and the yard had been dug up. "We were looking for the clean-out valve," said the

repairmen. "We didn't want to bother you," they explained.
She did happen to know where the valve was located, and
she could have shown them. After several weeks of arguing
about who was to blame, the repairmen finally returned to
clean up the yard and repair the damage.

Barbara pulled up to the drive-up window at the bank to
deposit a check—something she had done with Sam many
times, but always with Sam making the deposit. She sat in
her car, confused and alone. A disembodied voice asked,
"Can I help you?" She saw a cylinder in the receptacle next
to her car window. She put her check in the box and placed
the cylinder on top of it, figuring it was there as a paper-
weight. "I didn't get your check," said the voice. "It's there,"
replied Barbara. "Put it inside the tube," instructed the
teller. Barbara did, but she replaced the tube flat in the box.
"Put it in upright," the teller instructed her. As Barbara left,
the voice followed her: "Don't drive off with the tube!"

Barbara headed for home, visibly shaken. Suddenly the
car began to lurch and sputter. The gas tank was empty!
Sam had always taken care of keeping the cars filled. Barbara pulled into a station where Sam had bought gas. She
got out of the car and looked at the gas pumps. Then she
walked around the car, trying to figure out where to put the
nozzle. She had no idea of how to pump the gas into her
car. Eventually she got the gas into her tank, but then she
realized she had no money. Fortunately, the gas station
accepted credit card charges; but as Barbara started her car
to drive away, the cashier called out to her, "Don't drive
away with the hose!"

Barbara's Predicament

Sam, the supposed "perfect husband," hid from his
own mortality and aging process. He neglected to teach
Barbara the practical things that women need to know. To

have given her the list for widows would have meant acknowledging his own mortality.

Barbara was equally to blame for her predicament. She had been happy to turn over the tasks she didn't like. Her ignorance of the practical world impacted at the worst possible time, when she was dealing with Sam's death.

Barbara is valiantly trying to make a comeback, but she is having difficulties. She doesn't sleep much at night, and although she does reach out more than in the past, part of her holds back from inexperience and fear. The push-pull leaves her exhausted. What a difference it would have made if she had begun to work on assertiveness and dependency issues sooner! Barbara is sixty-nine years old now, and recently she developed a heart condition. "If I had known I was going to live so long," she commented, "I would have taken better care of myself."

STRATEGIES TO OUTWIT AGING

Janet, Barbara, and the thousands of women like them, illustrate the importance of starting early campaign strategies to outwit aging. They also illustrate several circumstances that interfere with achieving a happier later life.

1. The advantage of recognizing aging as a "crisis" earlier would have resulted in more planning and reaching out in new directions. Both Janet and Barbara were "fortunate" in their early years, protected and insulated from change. They never experienced the crises that might have enabled them to start changing while there was still plenty of time.

2. Both let themselves be satisfied with the status quo instead of questioning the values in their lives. Janet especially worked hard at trying to hold onto the status quo—and this was her undoing.

3. Both women placed too much reliance on certain relationships. They used those relationships as a source of
self-esteem instead of developing their own internal resources. Janet didn't make an effort to reach out and
form new relationships. Barbara did, but she was handicapped by collusion with her husband and her envious
friends. If she had realized the implications, she might
have worked to develop more special activities for
herself.

Developing inner strength and, at the same time, some
social skills, combined with a new life's purpose, *will* make a
difference!

CHAPTER FIVE

The Inward Journey

When your present world is completely different from the world you were prepared for and your ways of responding to it are given little or no reinforcement, clearly it's time for you to change. It won't be easy; you've spent fifty or sixty years responding in the old ways. To change now will take a sizable commitment. But as we contemplate change, it's reassuring to know that today life offers us more solutions than problems. If we are a generation that was "done in" (as one woman put it) with society's conflicting expectations and pressures, we are also a generation with more opportunities for growth and expansion than any other. Inner awareness is a key to that growth and expansion.

In looking inward, we may discover that our values are changing. If the old values no longer work for us, this can be the time to set new, more basic, goals.

Aging beautifully, in a society that considers those words contradictory, is a demanding, creative endeavor. Physical beauty—at least, the kind touted by television—can be exchanged for inner beauty. The rewards of achievement can be traded for those of culture and wisdom. Power can be dropped in favor of intellectual interests or volunteer work that affects your environment in more personally rewarding ways.

AM I WHO SOCIETY SAYS I AM?

The first step on the inward journey is to discover the answer to this basic question: *Who am I?*

It's important to realize that who you are is separate from society's concept of *what* you are. In our culture, where twenty-eight-year-old television commentators seem to reign, it's easy for women—and men—over fifty to feel "old hat." This is natural; we tend to be who we are partly from the way other people perceive us. We define ourselves in terms set down by our environment. But this is the time to curb that tendency. "Who am I?" must come from within.

One of society's essential criteria seems to be how successful we are. But how is success defined? Is it through achievement that earns money? If we are hanging on to the financial value of achievement, we probably will become frustrated as we grow older and our energies diminish. But sometimes a new achievement goal can emerge, one that is not necessarily rewarded by a commercial society but still is an achievement.

Perhaps you never had a career outside the home. Does that mean you're a failure? It is time for us, and society as well, to refine its measures of success. No career? Clare Toth, psychologist, says, "Living is a career, and the only important one." Whether you are in the conventional achievement world or not, success should not be merely an "ego trip," something that inflates one's sense of importance. True success, Leonard Felder tells writers, is not in getting published; it is in "feeling that you've done something of value, that you've worked hard and reached some people in a helpful way." Often, work that disregards the materialistic goals does produce that success.

As we grow older, a realignment of what is really important seems to occur. Material success is seen as shallow. Finally it comes down to "who you are," not "who you know" or what you have been in the past.

Psychotherapists used to believe that older people had difficulty redefining themselves, since for years people defined themselves in terms of traditional roles that now are slipping away. Actually, many people do an excellent job of redefining themselves and are satisfied with their lives.

With maturity, approval comes from within. This is where it should have come from all along. As younger women, we conformed to society's expectations and relished the approval. We might miss the approval, but now we are free to feel good about who we are and what we do. Not expecting our validation to come only from someone else is essential.

DO I NEED A PERSONALITY CHANGE?

Many women who now are middle aged grew up unsure and shy. They were raised to think of themselves "not first, but sixth or maybe eighty-sixth," says Clare Toth. "Husbands, children, employers, friends, clients, community, starving children in India—just about everyone's needs were more important, we were told."

With new awareness that their needs are important, too, women today are changing their personalities. Most of the women I talked with who have achieved fulfillment made this change a priority. If they had been outgoing people who were accustomed to reacting quickly to people and places, they realized that they needed to develop the skills of reflection and conceptualization. They sought the inner wisdom that aging introverts often have. If they were people who had always looked inward, they realized that they needed to develop the ability to reach out and become more assertive. They recognized that although they may have fine ideas, noble thoughts, or warm affection, somehow they have been unable to communicate this to others. Now at late middle age, they see that it would be nice to be at least a little more outgoing so they could move more easily through life.

The process of change is stimulated by seeing that by middle age other people are enjoying the fruits of whatever qualities one lacks. The extrovert who may have appeared "pushy" and shallow now is in a position of influence. The shy bookworm has developed a depth of understanding that enriches her life. Seeing their rewards provides us with incentive to be more like these people. Jungian psychotherapists Janice Brewi and Anne Brennan discuss this tendency in their book, *Celebrate Mid-Life*.

The Rewards of Change

Joyce Marksell, a high school teacher now turning sixty, recalls that when she was fifty she felt invisible. Her husband's gray hair looked distinguished; hers looked dull. People no longer seemed interested in what she had to say. Who was she now? Not an energetic young beauty, not a wise old woman, just someone adrift. Then Joyce made a commitment to change. She turned within to discover who she was, what her values were. Once she had redefined herself, Joyce was able to shed the old roles and expectations. She was free to expand in new directions. Joyce enrolled in a class for beginning artists, and she discovered an untapped resource for growth. Today, at sixty, she feels positive about herself. She has made new friends and developed new interests. Her hair is almost white, but she feels vibrant and alive again—and "visible."

Shirley Campbell, a research psychologist, comments on this common experience of identity crisis in late middle age, followed by a happier adjustment. When you know who you are, you are comfortable with yourself. This self-awareness seems also to bring a new ability to be at ease with others, and those others seem to be more comfortable with you, too. Added to this, the new work and activity that women discover for themselves is fresh and stimulating and it enriches their lives.

FINDING A NEW PURPOSE FOR YOUR LIFE

When Ruth Gardner retired from teaching at the university, she realized two things: that work had formed the structure of her time, and that most of her activities had been organized from outside rather than from within herself. She wondered what she really wanted to do with the rest of her life. Ruth determined to take the example of E. B. White, author of My Year, in which he described his adventures as he followed his own inclinations. Ruth is reading the books she always wanted to read, and she writes. She is studying the work of Carl Jung, with a special interest in his philosophy about the inward journey of the second half of life. At times her concentration is disrupted by the real-life concerns that can occur at this time of life—her health, the health of an aging parent, household maintenance. Husband, children, and grandchildren keep her busy with happy interruptions. Nevertheless, she believes she is making steady progress in uncovering her true life goal. She has delayed making decisions about courses, volunteer work, and other community involvement until Her Year is over and her focus is set.

"My Month"

It might be hard for you to devote an entire year to self-discovery; there are so many family matters that impact. But My Month might be possible! Most family, social, volunteer, educational, travel, and recreational goals can be put on hold for thirty days.

For that one month, be introspective and hedonistic. Whenever possible, let go of things you are supposed to do. Don't let the cat starve, but skip anything extra. Read books, papers, magazines. Talk to friends about their activities, try out different community groups, meet new people, watch television shamelessly. Turn off restricting thoughts about "I could never do that" or "I really should help out with the church bazaar." This thirty-day period needs to be a noncritical and nonlimiting time to look at yourself and the world.

Observe your reactions to all the subjects and activities introduced. Watch for a feeling of pleasure, of wanting some continued connection. You may be out of touch with experiencing excitement, so look for subtle clues like feeling warm, relaxed, curious. When you find yourself reacting with even a twinge of excitement, make a note of what brought on the interest. Later, look at your list.

Childhood Clues

What did you want to be when you were a little girl—before someone told you it wasn't possible, that you couldn't do it, that no one makes money doing it? Write down two of your childhood dreams, and think about what you could do today to fulfill them.

Did you like to play house, dance, play hospital, write poems, swing on a trapeze, play with animals? All of these memories are additional clues to finding the interest that will bring you happiness. Did you prefer to do things alone or with others? Did you like to organize things, create? This can be a clue not only to what you like to do, but what kind of setting you enjoy. Some people value autonomy above all else, others like to be one of a cooperative group, others like to organize people and activities rather than to do the activity itself.

Brainstorming

Brainstorm for ideas on how you could develop particular interests. Say you had once served as a juror and had found the courtroom scene meaningful. Is it too late to be a lawyer? Not necessarily. If you decide that it *is* too late, think of other ways you can be involved in the law. The courts might need people to help juvenile offenders with home studies. You could join the League of Women Voters and work on projects that help to improve the legal system. You might want to visit or teach in the jails.

The drama at the local community theatre "turned you on"—but heavens, it's too late to become an actress. Not so! Acting is one field in which age is not a limitation, and acting classes are for students of all ages. It's hard to make it on Broadway or in Hollywood as a new actor; but local theatres always need older actors, and many seniors are acting in commercials produced locally and nationally. A successful actress told me, "It's better for older actors. We have been acting for years and are getting burned out. The older woman can approach her acting with a fresher mind set."

Extending the Month

If you haven't found the right activity by the end of Your Month, give yourself another month. Just be sure to take every opportunity to delve into your inner self. Resist the temptation to keep going on the same comfortable track—unless you are absolutely sure it is the right track for you. Say yes to all new ideas, all fresh ways of looking at old ideas. When you discover the right combination of idea and direction, you'll know it. Recognizing that combination can transform your life.

TAKING CHARGE OF YOUR HEALTH

All transformations take place more readily when you feel well and have the energy to do what you want to do.

Happily aging women say they take charge of their physical health. They consult physicians, but they take responsibility for making healthful living choices. They combine advice from various sources with listening to the clues their own bodies give. Many books are designed to guide women in taking care of their health. Of course, common sense must be used. The body that shifts too quickly from red meat every night to a diet of beans and sprouts may run into problems. Any major change in eating habits or level of exercise must be checked out with a physician.

In Chapter 9, we will take a closer look at our health care, our doctors, and our responsibilities to both.

Exercise

The body is designed for motion. We feel better and stay healthier when we find some way to exercise. But exercise does more than improve physical health; it also invigorates the mind, gives release to the emotions, and brings confidence to the personality.

Walking and swimming are preferred exercises for older adults. There are organized exercise programs available in every community. For those who are unable to take part in vigorous programs, there are many options. Water exercise is one choice, and "splash dancing" classes are another. In both, water supports most of the body weight. The muscles are exercised and circulation is stimulated with less stress to the joints. Check your local Arthritis Foundation, hospitals, and community recreation centers for information about these programs.

Stress and Prescription Drugs

Physicians have been telling us for years that stress causes many of our physical problems, but they are just beginning to understand how to alleviate that stress.

A number of women told me how much they regretted taking the tranquilizers that doctors used to prescribe routinely for tension. Valium and Librium are useful drugs, good to have in a crisis. When a woman takes them habitually as a solution for stress, however, eventually she may find that she doesn't function very well and the drugs haven't helped her to resolve the problems that led to the stress.

In former years another commonly prescribed drug for women was Desoxyn. It was an amphetamine ("speed") prescribed for weight loss and depression. Weary housewives were glad to have it to get through the day. But for many women who had gone through an amphetamine day, a tranquilizer was a "must" in order to get any rest at night. Jean Harris, the former director of a girls' school who shot her lover, the celebrated Scarsdale Diet Doctor, Herman Tarnower, took medically prescribed amphetamines for ten years. She believes the drugs had a part in raveling her depressed personality to contemplate suicide. She claims that it was her suicide attempt gone wrong, rather than murder, that ended Dr. Tarnower's life.

This extreme case reminds us how casually drugs were given to women thirty-some years ago, at the very time that the women who are now in their fifties were beginning the responsibilities of adult life. Why women? No answer, other than the fact that healthy young women were more apt to enter the medical system via their pregnancies. Until Betty Friedan's book, *The Feminine Mystique*, was widely read in the 1960s, the stress of being a housewife and mother was not fully appreciated. A distressed woman was considered neurotic. Her complaints were discounted and the drugs soothed her nerves. With increased awareness of side effects and long-term problems, this kind of prescription drug usage has been largely discontinued.

New Ways to Deal with Stress

Alternative therapies become an important part of health care after fifty. Many of the "holistic" or alternative modalities are designed to relieve stress. Biofeedback, transcendental meditation, t'ai chi, yoga, Jin Shin Jyutsu, therapeutic massage, autogenics, self-hypnosis, all help with calming and soothing. Many teachers of these methods also work with their clients to recognize and alleviate the life difficulties that are causing the stress. Psychotherapists, self-help books, workshops, and support groups deal with methods to curb the accumulating stress in the first place.

Physicians may be uneasy about alternative methods; they have been trained to need scientific proof before recommending a particular treatment. Orme-Johnson, Ph.D., writing in *Psychosomatic Medicine*, describes research to establish that proof. Dr. Orme-Johnson is chairman of the psychology department at the Maharishi International University. He reports the results of a five-year analysis of statistics on medical insurance use. The insurance company, MIC, is a major medical carrier with members nationwide. In Orme-Johnson's study, the use of medical inpatient and outpatient care was contrasted between regular MIC users and members of a subgroup called SCI. To belong to SCI, there are two special requirements: that the policyholder and all family members practice transcendental meditation techniques regularly for six months prior to enrollment, and that they continue the regular practice of this form of relaxation for fifteen to twenty minutes twice a day. The age groups and types of illnesses represented in Dr. Orme-Johnson's study were broad and inclusive. Actuaries compared the results of other major medical carriers with the SCI group. The patients who practiced transcendental meditation had significantly lower rates of illness. In the five years analyzed, there were 55.4 percent fewer hospital admissions for cancer, 87.2 percent fewer for heart disease, 30.4 percent fewer for infections, and 30.6 percent fewer for all types of mental disorders.

Although this study dealt with transcendental meditation, some other therapies can be substituted. Biogenics, autogenics, self-hypnotism, and relaxation therapy all involve the use of the alpha consciousness, a calm center that produces relaxation.

A Harvard study resulted in similar conclusions. Dr. Joan Borysenko was a cell biologist at Harvard. She joined Dr. Herbert Benson, a cardiologist, who was researching the effects of meditation and visual imagery on physical illness. Dr. Benson believes that relaxation therapy can be used as both a treatment and a preventive strategy for all illnesses that have a known connection with stress. Those disorders include chronic pain, low back pain, heart and circulation problems, colitis, ulcer, and arthritis. Other illnesses, including cancer, are not as specifically related to stress and need further research. That research is taking place in continuing clinical studies.

Many of the illnesses that accompany aging are chronic. They are not open to an all-out cure, but are amenable to techniques like these that at least can help one function. One can have various physical problems, yet still have a feeling of well-being and enjoy a good quality of life.

It is important to combine the use of alternative care with traditional medicine. Although the alternative therapies are safe, there is a risk of getting carried away with this new world of possibilities. People have died by sticking with the New Age therapies and neglecting to check in with their regular doctor.

When using one of the alternative methods, be sure to start out with a recognized therapist, not just someone who took a workshop. There are organizations that exist specifically to establish standards for care and train biofeedback operators and other therapists. While the techniques are simple, supervision is important in the early stages. A person who is tight from years of tension may relax so suddenly at a biofeedback session that light-headedness will occur. After the initial treatments, the patient can continue the technique independently, sometimes guided by audiotaped instructions.

Medical insurance usually does not cover the cost of alternative therapies unless they are referred by a physician. The ideal situation is to find a doctor who works with holistic therapists. The primary care physician then can monitor the effects.

BUILDING SELF-ESTEEM

Helen Briggs was an assistant professor at the Graduate School of Social Work at the University of Kansas.

Now retired from that position, she continues to give workshops in self-esteem and family dynamics. Helen believes that self-esteem is the key to growth at any age. "Many people don't realize how low their self-esteem may be. They pass through life feeling depressed, not realizing that there is any other way to feel. Usually these people have not been given the kind of positive reinforcement that would enable them to feel good and to grow emotionally. In the past, our society hasn't encouraged children to feel good about themselves. Without a positive self-image, it is very difficult to be inquisitive and assertive."

The best situation is to have come from a home where nurturing parents encouraged self-confidence—a feeling of being special and important. That self-confidence then can be carried into the crises of adult life. If you don't have it now, Helen Briggs believes, you can consciously work to develop it.

Here are seven direct and immediate steps that can help you increase your self-esteem.

Helen's Exercise

Take out a sheet of paper and a pen. Quickly make a list of your good qualities. Read it over. Now list some more. If you stumble over this exercise, or if your list is embarrassingly short, turn to page 94 and read Helen's word list for expanding your self-image. See how many of those qualities apply to *you*. Add them to your list. Review Helen's list every week, and continue to add new qualities to your list as you grow in self-esteem.

Don't peek at the list yet—write your list first!

Tapes and Books

There are many published materials that teach the self-appreciation that is necessary for us to move forward.

HELEN'S EXERCISE FOR EXPANDING YOUR SELF-IMAGE

able	good cook	progressive
accepting	good friend	protective
adaptable	growing	proud
adventurous	handsome	proud parent
ambitious	happy	rational
at ease	helpful	realistic
attractive	honorable	reasonable
authoritative	idealistic	reassuring
balanced	imaginative	reflective
bold	independent	relaxed
brave	ingenious	reliable
calm	innovative	religious
carefree	intelligent	resolute
caring	intuitive	resourceful
certain	jovial	respectful
cheerful	kind	responsible
chic	knowledgeable	satisfied
clear-thinking	learned	scientific
concerned	liberal	searching
confident	lively	seeker
consistent	logical	self-assertive
controlled	loving	self-aware
courageous	loyal	sense of humor
decisive	mature	sensible
dedicated	merry	serious
dependable	modest	sexy
determined	motivated	sociable
dignified	mystical	spiritual
disciplined	natural	spontaneous
dreamy	nurturing	stable
dutiful	objective	strong
educated	observant	supportive
effervescent	open	sympathetic
efficient	organized	tactful
empathetic	original	tenacious
energetic	patient	tender
enthusiastic	perceptive	thoughtful
extroverted	persuasive	trusting
fair	playful	trustworthy
flexible	pleasant	unassuming
frank	poised	understanding
free	positive	useful
friendly	powerful	visionary
generous	pragmatic	warm
genial	precise	wise
gets things done	predictable	witty
giving	pretty	youthful

Now revise your list of assets, and observe your self-esteem rise.

Teachers of autogenics, self-hypnosis, and other relaxation therapies often prepare individualized audiotapes for their students. Those same therapists can make tapes that are specifically designed to improve self-esteem.

Some general tapes and books on this subject are listed in the bibliography at the end of this book. Virginia Satir's book, *Self-Esteem*, has become a classic. Go to the library and check it out. While you're there, ask the librarian to recommend newly released audiotapes and books that encourage self-appreciation.

Self-Affirmations

Give thought to your own special qualities, and turn those thoughts into positive messages to yourself.

Therapists once thought that these affirmations were too superficial to be helpful. Now they are recognized as being powerful.

"I've tried affirmations," you may say, "and they didn't help *me* very much." Take a look at the ones you used. When they are too long and all-encompassing (as many printed affirmations tend to be), they may not really speak to your needs. Write your own immediate, brief, believable affirmations, and you will feel their power.

"Every woman," says Helen Briggs, "should start the day affirming something positive about herself." I have a friend who looks in her mirror every morning and says, "What a woman!"

Think of your own special needs for confidence, and create specific affirmations before you begin an activity, and afterward in praise and appreciation of yourself.

It is even more important to congratulate yourself at the end of each day. "I wrote an insightful poem. . . . I gave a marvelous dinner party." A person with phobias might say, "Today I drove the car across a bridge" or "I managed to go shopping this afternoon." Marvelous! For that person, it may have taken as much courage to walk out her front door as it did for Neil Armstrong to step out onto the moon.

Monitoring Negative Thoughts

Our minds are ever busy, carrying on a constant inner dialogue. That inner dialogue is made up of thoughts, impressions, and feelings—many of them self-defeating. Do they have to be? Most of us have a lot of "downer" messages from the past. You may need a grand sweep of them before the new positive affirmations can take hold. In their book, *The Inner Enemy*, Bach and Torbet describe negative dialogue. This enemy is like a museum curator. It keeps all the joyless, negative information in a file and can produce it at a moment's notice. Untrammeled, it can interfere with our capacity for enjoying life. ("Don't you remember how terrified you were on that last boat trip? You'd better turn down that invitation to go boating now!")

Bach suggests that we combat the Enemy with an Ally. In a fair fight, both sides are represented equally. The Ally can speak up to the negative Enemy by saying something positive.

Enemy: You look terrible.
Ally: I have many attractive features.
Enemy: People don't like me.
Ally: I am a fine person. Many people like me very much.

Another technique is to deliberately recall things that make you feel happy—an event, a song, a mountain view. To give yourself help in recalling those happy moments, place favorite pictures where you can see them, and play your favorite music often.

To combat the negative more intensely, consider joining a group such as a Course in Miracles. This is an ongoing nondenominational program that offers support and a unique educational approach to human difficulties. The "miracle" is your own transformation and resultant positive response from your environment as you develop positive attitudes. Although the program has a spiritual orientation, no particular religious creed is promoted. The philosophy blends psychology with spirituality of the Eastern religions and Christianity. Usually there is no cost other than the purchase of a textbook, and it is not necessary to belong to the sponsoring church. Religious organizations that sponsor these programs include the Unity Church (an international denomination) and many Methodist churches.

Attitudinal Healing is another nationwide network of support groups for personal growth and change. Attitudinal Healing is the process of letting go of painful and fearful attitudes, and thereby promoting growth and healing. The process grew out of a program to help children with catastrophic illnesses find support and a personal growth that would give them inner peace and a feeling of well-being. The program expanded to adults with illnesses, and it is now available to people who are not clinically ill but wish to achieve a feeling of well-being that is "health." There are Attitudinal Healing centers in many cities. The cost of the program is low or nonexistent. Contact the national center for information: Center for Attitudinal Healing, 19 Main Street, Tiburon, California 94920, Telephone: (415) 435-5022.

In order to combat negative thoughts, many people need to avoid others who give them destructive messages, even if these people are relatives (as indeed they often are). Some people choose to no longer watch catastrophes on the television news.

Deep-seated negativity is difficult to do away with completely. However, these techniques do help people to avoid dwelling on the negative thoughts and letting nonproductive feelings keep them from getting on with positive living.

Freedom from the Judgment of Others

Rose Tennant, M.D., is a pathologist who became a stress therapist. She believes that low self-esteem is the result of fear. "Children learn to please others in order to protect themselves from criticism and anger," she explains. "When you are little and all the big people in the world are controlling you, you have to say yes all the time. In school, you have to say yes again. There comes a time when you have to see through the whole game of yes and pleasing. It means your identity is coming from whether people like you or not, whether they approve of you or not. Your identity has nothing to do with what people think of you. Your identity comes from God, or the Creator, *because you are alive!* The opinions and judgments of other people have nothing to do with who you are. This game of please is full of fear and guilt. Now, if you really see that, you can begin to move into an area where you begin to say no to people who are trying to take your life and make you conform to their wishes."

Progressive Relaxation

Relaxation techniques can be combined with appreciation for the body that has brought you so far in life. The exercise below uses a concept of relaxation and self-esteem similar to that which Louise Hay wrote about in her book, *Love Your Body.* When used during physical discomforts, it is a pleasant reminder that the rest of the body is healthy.

Beth's Exercise   Lie down on the floor. Consciously relax all the muscles of the body. Talk to each part as you relax it.

My feet! How marvelous you are, carrying me for all these years, bearing my weight and making it possible for me to move about on this beautiful earth.

My legs! How strong you have been, enabling me to walk, to run, to dance. Thank you for the joy of movement.

My abdomen! I appreciate the lovely sexual feelings you have brought, the bearing of my children, the elimination of toxic substances from my body. How well you have served me.

My chest! I appreciate the breath of life and the power of my heart and arteries to carry the oxygen I need to every part of my body.

My jaw, my mouth! You enable me to enjoy food, to talk, to share my thoughts with others.

My ears! Through you I hear, and I am connected with the world.

My eyes! I thank you for showing me the world's beauty.

My mind, so keen and interested! You are the source of my well-being.

My spirit, the essential of my being! How I appreciate your strength.

Use this self-appreciation exercise, and see how good you feel! Give special love and appreciation to a body part that is not doing well. It has done its job for many years, and it may do so again.

Breathing Techniques

Breathing techniques have been used for centuries by Eastern seekers of health and positive mental changes. Beata Jencks, Ph.D., a psychology instructor at the University of Utah, has developed many breathing techniques. She cautions that we Westerners are by nature more tense than our Eastern counterparts, and we need to be more cautious lest breathing exercises increase tension. The out breath is especially important. She combines breathing with visualization. The in breath gives energy, is stimulating; the out breath gives the needed relaxation.

The following adaptation of one of her exercises is useful for increasing self-esteem.

1. Relax tense muscles—all of them.
2. Breathe in, visualizing "energy, confident."
3. Breathe out, visualizing "relaxed pleasure."
4. Allow a pause after each breath to observe reactions.

Do this breathing exercise only twice at one sitting.

FINDING HARMONY WITH THE UNIVERSE

As they grow older, many women who are not religious in the traditional sense often begin to feel a certain unity with the world and with others. They come to sense that other people represent parts of one's past or parts of oneself.

The Apache ceremony of Changing Woman reflects this philosophy of unity. At puberty, a young Indian girl is surrounded by family and friends in a ceremony that lasts for several days. A medicine man presides, along with an older woman who becomes the girl's sponsor. The young girl wears a white or gray eagle feather in her hair, ensuring that she will live until her hair turns a similar color. The girl dances on buckskin, lightly bouncing on one foot and then the other to the beat of the drums. The buckskin symbolizes a plentiful supply of meat and signifies that the girl will never know hunger.

During the ceremony, the young girl is transformed into a mythological being called Changing Woman. Special dances and chants ensure that she will pass through all the seasons of her life, and she is given the cane she will carry when she is an old woman. By symbolically passing into old age, she ensures her own long life. The power of Changing Woman enters her body.

This meeting of the stages of life is reflected in a less mystical way by a poem written by my daughter, Gwen McConnell, when she was fifteen.

Walking Opposite

A woman walking on opposite sidewalk
In gray. Too old to understand the way
I am, the way youth is. Covered in gray,
The gray she hides in beauty parlor talk.
Middle-aged and jealous of my young walk.
Pity the old, pity the gray. I say
"Hello," and I pity the woman in gray.

Woman in gray returns "Hello." The clock
Pities the young girl walking opposite.
Too young to understand the way I am,
The way life is. Too young to know the truth
Experience provides. Too young to quit,
Her energy will try to understand
The love, the pain, the clock. Pity the youth.

Spirituality at Midlife

"I don't go to church and I don't go for this new spiritual movement," says Rachel Zane, "but I do believe there is some sort of perception we humans have that we don't yet know about. I've seen so many times where people have the same idea in different parts of the country, different parts of the world. It's as if there's something in the air."

The new spirituality that many people experience at fifty or sixty is not necessarily the kind of spirituality that comes from attending church. For some people, conventional religion seems to be counterproductive to spirituality because it can create fears and anxieties about doing "the right thing." Others find their formal religious practice helps them to grow and expand at this time of life, and they increase their involvement in organized religion. It seems to depend, in part, on the particular church or organization and how oriented it is toward personal spiritual understanding.

What, then, is "spirituality," defined not in the usual way but as it pertains to the woman wanting to find peace with the universe? It is a feeling that the world is basically beautiful and filled with wonder; that there is a dimension of life beyond what is known, through either theology or science; and that the universe, and the divine power that creates and maintains it, can be trusted. It is a belief that there is spiritual meaning in one's life, whether that life is happy or sad; and that by looking inward, we can learn to understand and accept our experiences. There may be much in our lives that frustrates and impedes, many losses and disappointments. Yet these events are interpreted as lessons we need to learn for our growth, and are in fact meant to be.

If "the proof is in the pudding," it does seem that women who have this philosophy, whether or not they also have traditional religious beliefs, do find meaning in their lives and are marvelously relaxed about it.

Meditation

Meditation is a simple technique to produce a relaxation response and a deep peace of mind. The altered state of mind has been an important part of Indian culture for thousands of years. It is an old yoga practice that brings about a union of the self with a Supreme Being. The Western religions also have a meditative background.

While meditation has a spiritual element, it need not be used for that purpose only. Many people meditate to lower their blood pressure or just to stay calm. Studying transcendental meditation helps, but meditation can be done on your own. Here is one method.

1. Sit comfortably, with feet on the floor and eyes closed. A quiet environment is needed.
2. Deeply relax all your muscles, beginning at your feet and moving up to the muscles of the face and scalp.
3. Become conscious of your breath. Say "Om" when you inhale and exhale (or say "One" if you don't wish to identify with the Indian tradition). If you have taken transcendental meditation classes, you will have your own mantra.
4. Allow distracting thoughts to enter your mind, but in a passive way; and allow them to leave and keep returning to the sound.
5. A deep relaxation will take place. (It may take practice, but it will come.) Open your eyes after twenty minutes. Glance at the clock now and then, rather than set an alarm.

Meditation twice a day, not right after meals, will produce greater states of relaxation and an increased sense of well-being.

Body/Mind Therapy

Muriel Carlson followed the traditional path—marriage, family, and training for a career in psychology.

Now that she is in her fifties she has added a new dimension of spirituality and body/mind work by studying Jin Shin Jyutsu. This ancient body technique for harmonizing body, mind, and spirit is based on established principles of acupressure. Recently Muriel retired from her position as a school counselor and began a new career as a Jin Shin therapist. Muriel says, "When we learn to feel a part of a loving universe and we experience that harmony, we have a clearer sense of our life's purpose. We already know that purpose; we just have to get in touch with it. The universe is always there, always supporting us. We are so busy with our own agenda, we don't usually listen."

Breathing is an important technique, Muriel advises. Most people breathe from their upper chests, but we need to draw breath from lower in the body, around the navel. "To draw on the greatest amount of divine energy, to get into the breath and then exhale all our sorrows, is transforming," says Muriel.

Autogenics

Autogenics is a form of deep relaxation, similar to medical hypnosis and meditation techniques. This altered state of mind normalizes the autonomic nervous system, the part of the nervous system that becomes tense with stress. Both body and mind relax, and anxieties vanish. Part of the therapy requires the patient to recall emotions that are troublesome, express them openly, and learn other ways of looking at them.

Rose Tennant, M.D., an autogenics therapist, says this approach is especially appropriate for those over fifty because it teaches one how to deal with loss and change.

"Loss and change go hand in hand," says Dr. Tennant.

"When you have one, you usually have the other. Life is made up of a series of problems: 'I had an accident. . . . I lost my husband. . . . I got sick and couldn't work.' Sometimes we stress ourselves with resistance: 'How can this be? Why me?' We need to learn to accept the changes in life.

"You have to realize that nothing is stable," Dr. Tennant continues. "But there is something in you that doesn't change. You are not just this body. You *are* this world of change, and you also are your spirit. You are the learner, not the things that you learned. Speaking English or Italian, being a Republican or a Democrat, a doctor or a fire chief, being good or bad—these attributes are acquired. They are not who you are.

"We exist on two levels," she continues. "The body is in the world, on the physical level. But the world is as you interpret it in your mind. The physical level of life changes, but the essential mind does not. Understanding this helps us to deal with changes and loss.

"The older body has been here for many years. It is full of memories and, therefore, emotions—many of them unpleasant. We are taught as children to control feelings, to push them down. So we pile up negative feelings inside. By recognizing and releasing those painful feelings, we restore health to both the mind and the body.

"The true mind is always present in space. What to do with past suffering? Observe it, express it, and let it go. It is in the past, and is not part of the true, essential mind and spirit.

"Comparing ourselves to others is destructive," says Dr. Tennant. "We're like apples on a tree, and no two apples are the same. Over here is a peach tree, and here is a plum tree. Now, if I'm trying to be a peach instead of an apple, I can't even be a good apple. That's competition. But I have to remember that the apples come from one root system, and the peaches come from another root system, and so do the plums—but all the root systems come from one source. We are all one. We don't always see that. We just see conflict, separation, and this bad thing that is happening to 'poor little me.' If we see that underlying unity, we don't feel victimized."

At thirty-six, Dr. Tennant was herself a "victim" of stress. She was practicing pathology in her own laboratory for sixteen hours a day. She had contracts with three hospitals, and she had five people under her direction. Her mother was critically ill, and Rose was giving her medical treatment at home.

Overwhelmed and exhausted, she fell across the bed one night. "If this is what life is about," she thought, "I don't want to live." At that moment, she heard a voice inside her head: "You created it, you change it." She realized that she was blaming the world for what she was feeling. She wasn't taking responsibility for her part in it. Rose sold the laboratory and took a year off to care for her mother and heal herself.

After her mother died, Rose returned to the pathology laboratory. But after experiencing a more centered, healthful way of life, she found that now she viewed the medical world differently. She had wanted to be a physician in order to heal. Was the elaborate medical system of medications and surgeries really curing many illnesses? Medicine saves lives when illnesses are acute. But the major health problems of our society have become the chronic dysfunctions that are not so easily cured. She believed that relaxation and its related therapies are the true healers and that medicine should be used more appropriately to prevent and ameliorate illness. She wondered about her calling, and eventually she changed her specialization from pathology to stress management.

SETTLING UNFINISHED BUSINESS WITH PARENTS

Gypsy Lyle is a social worker who heads a women's recovery program in an inpatient hospital. She says, "These later midlife years are hard. You're still finishing up old things—your work, children in college, parents who are aging. Yet you have this issue of growing older and needing to find a new identity yourself. To get on with it, a woman needs to resolve old hurts and resentments with her parents. It may be easier now, since maturity itself increases understanding and compassion. Also, experience in being a parent teaches us how very hard it is to be one."

Many adult daughters are involved with caring for a difficult aging parent or visiting a parent frequently in a nursing home. To be involved in those ways without having resolved old issues is to court emotional disaster.

Who would think women of sixty and seventy would remain deeply distressed about the relationship with their parents? We must remember that parents of that older generation were afraid of spoiling their children, and they tended to be overcritical. Distress may be intensified as their mature children begin to recap their lives in an effort to find meaning and significance. Most of us grew up in families in which it was not okay for children to get angry. ("How can you talk to your mother like that! . . . After all we did for you!") So we stuff the feelings deep inside for a lifetime.

Dr. Harold Bloomfield, director of psychiatry at a wellness center in California, explains that wherever there is intense love, there also is intense anger. And since people and situations will always resemble past circumstances, we are continually reminded of our feelings. In his book, *Making Peace with Your Parents*, Dr. Bloomfield suggests a five-part solution to dealing with these old issues.

1. Accept your feelings.

2. Express those feelings in a long letter to each of your parents (never to be sent!), or in a serious conversation with a close friend, or to a therapist or in a group.

3. Then—and only then—*let your resentments go.* It is releasing to forgive your parents.

   It may help you to do so if you acknowledge the situations and feelings that may have influenced them. Chances are, they were not able to give you what you needed when you needed it because they were affected by something or someone else at the time. Perhaps that someone was you! If it was, forgive yourself for whatever negative part you played in the relationship.

4. Experience the loving feelings that now come to you, and openly express those positive feelings.

5. Become your own parent. Learn self-nourishing techniques and attitudes that provide the kind of acceptance and love you always wanted from them.

In *The Wounded Woman,* Linda Leonard writes eloquently about patriarchal authoritarian attitudes. Those attitudes devalued feminine qualities and prevented women's creative growth. After experiencing the rage and the tears of the father-daughter relationship, Linda Leonard says, "It is important to begin the healing. We need to reclaim our fathers." We list the hurtful qualities our fathers have or had (authoritativeness, absence, intimidation) and the positive qualities that they represent (strength, decisiveness, adventure). In this way, we can claim not only them but ourselves. In rejecting the negative qualities, Leonard believes we also reject the positive ones, not only in our fathers but in ourselves; and these are the very qualities we need for a successful life.

It is important to follow these same steps in making peace with parents who are no longer living. They are still a part of you, and the process is just as important. If the metaphysical people are correct, there is a spiritual connection with those who have died. They have not ceased to be, but merely have crossed over to another dimension. Now it may be easier to feel closer to that parent.

COUNSELING AND PSYCHOTHERAPY

Reframing Your Life

Psychiatric nurse and therapist Areta Johnson sees many women who are divorced, widowed, and defeated by disappointments. She believes that group treatment helps these women to realize they are not alone, that many people suffer the same losses. Instead of looking at their losses as disasters, they learn that "this is living." It's all right to be sad; in fact it is necessary to mourn losses. But it is not necessary to become deeply depressed over something that happens to many people and is part of the flow of life.

Letting Go

Learning to let go of life's losses is vital to happiness. Expressing sadness over those losses is as important as letting go of the person or situation that is gone. Coming to terms with earlier losses may prepare us to deal with the losses that come later, during the years that bring illness and death of loved ones. You become "your own person" through this process, and you no longer require any particular other human being or life situation to meet your needs.

Letting go of "ego needs" like approval and applause, and looking inward instead of outward for your needs, results in an unexpected bonus—wisdom!

Wisdom is a quality of being that is in touch with the deeper realities of life. It erupts out of the chaos of midlife, when so many of our goals and dreams get a good shaking up. We are brought to an impasse, a frustration about what has not worked or what has been lost, and we begin to look within ourselves to find our true needs and goals. We seek answers to the big questions about the meaning of life and our personal life quests. We begin to observe patterns of experience, reflect on them, and find a unique meaning in them. We become aware in a spiritual sense that there is a true self that is growing and developing along with the other "ego" self. Finally, we see a larger reality, an enlarged concept about life and about ourselves. This new understanding is wisdom.

Before this exciting stage can be reached, a lot of work needs to be done. Experiences need to be sorted out and changes need to be made. A lot can be done on your own, but sometimes it's better to work with a psychotherapist.

The Psychotherapist's Role

Older people experience a great many losses and have various crises that temporarily knock out their ability to cope and adjust. An emotional boost, a caring approach from another person, can restore their natural ability to cope and to feel good about themselves.

Support is a part of all therapy. The therapist offers *empathy*, which is different from the *sympathy* offered by friends. In empathy, the other person communicates understanding of your concern at an emotional level. The sympathetic friend is feeling sorry for you and may be overidentifying. Empathetic support is more conducive to your growth.

The therapist also can help clients to confront ideas and behaviors that are limiting. At the same time, the therapist affirms personal strengths and helps clients to set new goals for change and increase self-confidence. The supportive therapist also puts clients in contact with agencies that provide more concrete kinds of help, such as nursing care and emergency shelters.

There are several traditional forms of counseling. We will look at several. Bear in mind, however, that it is more important to feel comfortable with the therapist and to get started in something than it is to be sure you are in the right methodology.

Cognitive Therapy

Areta Johnson believes that women over fifty do well with cognitive therapy, which concentrates on helping us look at the truth of the situation rather than permitting emotions to take over.

People can become miserable over beliefs and ideas that are inappropriate. By correcting those beliefs, we can free ourselves from the negative emotions those false beliefs have caused. We then can take charge of our lives. It is not considered necessary to go into the childhood roots of those negative impressions.

Life is rarely one way or the other to the degree that we perceive it. If we try to categorize every experience, we will have an inaccurate picture of the world—and the picture most likely will be negative. The negative thoughts feel "real," and so we think they are true and we become depressed. Bach and Torbet, authors of *The Inner Enemy*, identified four basic types of irrational thoughts that cause problems.

1. *Arbitrary inference.* "Sally didn't speak to me at the party. She must be angry." This could be an unwarranted conclusion. Sally might be ill or distracted.
2. *Overgeneralization.* "Bill didn't ask me out for a second date, and he didn't return my call." You see this as a personal affront, and you feel rejected. "I am never going to find a boyfriend. I am always going to be

lonely and miserable." These are thoughts that need not follow. One negative event does not foretell a never-ending pattern of defeat.

3. *Catastrophizing.* "Maybe I'm not attractive enough. If I were, Bill would have called." You begin to magnify your faults and minimize your strengths. At that point, you do become a loser—but only to your own thought processes.

4. *Selective abstraction.* "Sally found time to talk to Janet at the party. She likes Janet better than she likes me." In this kind of thinking, you pick up on a negative detail, dwell on it, and end up seeing the whole situation in a negative light. It is like a single drop of ink darkening a whole glass of water. Positive facets of the experience are filtered out so that you are aware only of the negative.

Cognitive therapy's concentration on the present is a plus for older people, since the causes of their unhappiness probably have been compounded by real-life traumatic events. The method is limited in time, which is another plus for older people who may not have the financial resources for long-term care.

Feeling Good, written by David D. Burns, M.D., is a useful self-help book that describes cognitive therapy techniques in detail.

Insight Therapy

In this traditional psychoanalytical therapy, the patient explores past emotional experiences. It is a most thorough overhaul of one's life and attitudes and a chance to reenact and resolve old relationships. Growth is experienced through the intense relationship that develops between client and therapist. In its classic form, insight therapy continues for several years. Modified forms have been developed, however, that require only a few months.

Psychoanalysis has an important place in helping to deal with past losses, a common problem with older people. When those past losses are especially painful, the analysis needs to be done with special care. Freud believed that anyone over fifty lacked flexibility of the ego and could not be analyzed. But psychiatrists now find that people are able to benefit from insight at any age. Psychoanalysis tells us that it is important to mourn our losses and then let them go, freeing up our energy for a new situation.

Transactional Analysis

Transactional analysis has the advantage of using simple words to express psychological concepts. This unique language helps people to both understand and change behavior. "TA" is down-to-earth, practical, and can be short-term or long, group or individual. Group therapy is considerably less expensive.

A transaction is an exchange, usually verbal, between two people—a unit of behavior. What happens in the transaction is analyzed, especially if it produces an unpleasant emotion like hurt or anger. All of us are three persons in one: sometimes the "Child" we used to be, sometimes a "Parent" in ways copied from our own parents, and sometimes "Adult." The Adult is objective, can solve problems. When people feel hurt, usually they have drifted into their Child, with the hurt triggered by something they see as Parental. Today's feelings can reflect old Parental "tapes." Learning to understand our responses and activate the problem-solving Adult can calm the hurt feelings. Both Parent and Child "tapes" are studied thoroughly, and new responses are learned.

As transactions are analyzed, the personality is gradually guided in a new direction. As a Child, we may have made pessimistic decisions about ourselves ("I'm no good"). What was decided then can be redecided now—this time in our own favor.

Treatment for Codependency and Other Addictions

Are you still wrapped up in other people's problems? Most women are. A husband has job difficulties or is an alcoholic, a child has behavior problems, a parent is ill. You can't help worrying and getting involved. How much of your energy is going into worry? When you talk to friends about your life, how much of the conversation is about the family member and the problem? Do you excuse your husband's moodiness because of his unhappy past? Do you become his therapist?

It is common for women to do all these things and to get into relationships that are "addictive" in that they can't leave them, no matter how much they jeopardize the woman's own well-being. It has to do with fear—fear of being alone, fear of not being loved. When men don't come through with love and support, women love all the more, try even harder. This process is called codependency.

Men have the same fears and feelings of inadequacy, but when they suppress them in addictions, it is usually to things in the outside world—alcohol, work, sports, whatever gives them a feeling of being okay. Women tend to focus directly on their need for love by overinvesting in their close relationships.

In her book, *Women Who Love Too Much*, Robin Norwood writes, "It is one of the ironies of life that we women can respond with such sympathy and understanding to the pain in one another's lives while remaining so blinded to (and by) the pain in our own." Women cannot avoid their own pain forever. It comes out, often at middle age, in tension and depression and poor health.

Is it possible to recover from such a pervasive problem? Yes, especially now that women are given definite guidelines for doing so. Ms. Norwood tells us that the woman who recovers is the one who accepts the fact that there is only one life that is within her control—her own life. The women who recover are not necessarily the ones whose situation is less serious, but they are the ones who take action and give change a priority. They are determined and they find support groups to help them recover.

Many women have been helped at Al-Anon meetings. Although originally intended to help spouses of alcoholics, Al-Anon groups now offer support to family members of those with other addictions—drugs, gambling, even sex.

The Adult Children groups sponsored by Al-Anon are an especially good resource for women who come from dysfunctional families. (Most of us can find an alcoholic or other addicted person in our parents' or grandparents' generation. Using the term *addiction* liberally to include workaholics, most families are covered!) The Al-Anon treatment is effective, and there is no fee. A hat is passed for voluntary contributions.

Look in the telephone directory for Al-Anon, or call Alcoholics Anonymous for information. In a town of any size, groups meet at different times of the day and in different parts of town.

Many communities are developing other codependency support groups. Check the free weekly newspapers. Look in church bulletins. Consult the bookstores that feature self-help and growth books. Some bookstores deal with addictions and codependency issues only.

BRANCHING OUT

No one will want to do—or have time to do—everything we have touched on in this chapter. Start wherever it seems right or whenever opportunities appear. Don't wait for the right teacher or the right guru to come along and get you going. The important thing is to get started! It will be easier to branch out once you have begun. Further transformation will be found out there in the world.

CHAPTER SIX

Reaching Out to the World

The art of living requires that we not only grow in ability to look within and affirm ourselves, but that we sharpen our skills for reaching outward to other people and to the community. This is a large order, until we realize that growth in the one area seeps into the other.

It is a difficult task for a man or woman who has always been introspective and reflective to start worrying about something so foreign as "group skills." If it hasn't been important before, why do we need to give it a thought now? Why not just leave us in peace?

There is a very practical reason: Growing older means facing an endless series of losses—beauty, health, money, loved ones; and depression frequently follows loss and change. Depression is the major emotional illness of people between sixty and sixty-five. These are the people who are most apt to be losing their employment, spouse, friends, homes, health, vigor, and hair. No wonder their stress levels are high!

People who stay depressed for a long period after a loss are more likely to be those who have fewer social skills. The socially aware person can more easily bring in new contacts to replace those that were lost. While loved ones cannot be replaced, new friends can be enjoyed. It is tragic and unnecessary to be unable to live without a certain human being and psychologically throw yourself on the funeral pyre.

But it is not enough merely to have an interest in the world. It is important to express it to other people. This practice improves social skills. It also improves your image. Society could easily mistake an older person's silence for indifference and boredom.

WHY THE OLD ROLES DON'T WORK

People are living longer, and the men and women who are now between middle age and old age represent a new phenomenon. We are educated, still energetic, and reasonably healthy; and society has no preordained role for us. In former societies, older women had roles as the purveyors of culture and the traditions. But today's young generation, swamped with an ever-changing flow of new ideas, doesn't dwell much on tradition.

It is futile to cling to the old roles. Clare Toth says, "I am no longer a mother" (that is, in the old sense of meeting the children's basic needs), "or it will destroy my children."

How about the role of wife? Mabel West gave up her personal interests and activities to be always available to her physician husband. Dr. Tom, now sixty, no longer needs her constant services. He wishes she would develop a life of her own, to take away some of the pressure on him to be everything to her. He really likes dining at the local restaurants more than staying home, and he would enjoy some time alone in the house. But he doesn't have the heart to tell her. Mabel would be shattered to find out that her lifelong sacrifice to him had been unnecessary and somewhat unappreciated.

And how about Grandma, the baker of chocolate-chip cookies and apple pies? Her role worked for a while—but then the grandchildren grew up and rejected cholesterol and sugar in favor of bean sprouts and tofu.

Work-related roles can diminish with mergers, early retirements, competition with younger workers, and a reluctance to hire anyone over fifty. As for the housewife, the large house is sold and home becomes an apartment, the children leave, the husband may leave in search of eternal youth, and the dog dies!

Obviously, we need to look beyond the roles that society has rewarded in the past. We need to give up the whole idea of "role" and design an individualized purpose for our life. The purpose will not be based on society's expectations but on our own interests and sense of who we are. It is a defeat and a victory at the same time, that we can finally let go and be ourselves.

It's Hard to Let Go

One reason it is so difficult to let go is that living a role takes so much energy, hard work, time, and persistence. You don't raise five children (or even one), be a community leader, hold a demanding job for thirty years, do anything major, without almost a tunnel-vision kind of dedication. Your success came with a price, and that price was the neglect of other interests and other sides of your personality. With so much invested in one of these roles, it's hard to give it up. The role may have been frustrating, but it was yours. It's like putting hundreds of dollars of repairs into an old car that still doesn't work. "Perhaps with a little more effort I can make it work after all," we think.

It is frightening to contemplate change. In the process, we may find out a lot about ourselves that we would just as soon not know. If we do find a new direction for our lives, do we really want to take the risks that may be required? Sarah Lerner, the wise grandmother who was traveling the world alone, said, "You need to take risks. You don't know the outcome. It doesn't matter. The important thing is to make your move."

By the age of fifty, often whatever we *haven't* done begins to look more and more appealing. The woman who has raised a family and kept a fine home now thinks she may have wanted to become a lawyer all along. She would have had a brilliant career, not an album of photos of children who have left home anyway. The lawyer, now fifty, wonders if her success has been worth all the single-minded effort. She has a luxurious apartment, satisfying work, a telephone that rings constantly. But she is deeply lonely. Was it really so important to give her energy to clients, many of whom repeated their delinquent tendencies anyway, instead of to children of her own who could have grown more surely from her influence?

Janice Brewi and Anne Brennan write about the person who has climbed to the top of the ladder and at middle age thinks it may have been the wrong ladder. Suddenly the other ladders look better. Unfortunately, at this point many men and women jump off the ladder and become beach bums. Instead of falling off, we can look around from the pinnacle of the ladder, and we can stand at the top and take a closer look at the other ladders. It is true, we missed something. But perhaps we can incorporate into our lives some of what we missed. We can change ourselves and forget about ladders.

The mistake here is to cling desperately to the ladder in panic. This fear of change leads to futile attempts to continue the roles that haven't worked. We boss the children and rant at the difficult husband in a last-ditch effort to control the situation through anger. We continue the nonproductive conflict at work in the hopes of somehow making things right.

SKILLS WOMEN NEED

Independent Living Skills

It is important to learn the practical skills of daily living. Remember Barbara, the woman who lost her husband and had never handled finances, pumped gas at the self-serve station, or dealt with repairmen? Barbara learned those survival skills eventually, but it was almost overwhelming to have to learn them at the same time she was recovering from a major loss. Let's realize that everyone can be in this situation in one way or another. If Sam had been the one left alone, he might not know how to cook, or he might have put his white shirts and red sweat pants in the same wash load and then had to wear pink shirts to the office.

Between nine million and fifteen million people in this country are financially illiterate. They have no idea how to spend money wisely, handle banking transactions, balance checkbooks, or plan investments and savings for the future. Not all of these people are older women; many are men whose wives take care of these matters, or young people on their first job.

Social Skills

1. *Interest in people.* A woman who is interested in people and is able to express that interest can have friends at any age. Majda Thurnher, Ph.D., is a psychologist in the Human Development and Aging Program at the University of California. She has studied middle-aged adults for many years, and she believes that this is the basic quality that ensures a happy life.

2. *Interest in the world.* Dr. Thurnher also believes that it is important to have interests beyond human relationships. A natural curiosity helps. "The world is a fascinating place," says Sarah Lerner, who recently returned from a ten-day trip to the Soviet Union. Before the trip, Sarah read everything she could about the cities she planned to visit. She learned to ask directions and say a few phrases in Russian. The trip was a stimulating experience—tiring for her, at eighty-four, but always interesting.

3. *The talking-listening balance.* There are some people who talk continuously and never listen. Others are listeners. The talkers need to be charismatic "grande dames" to get away with it; otherwise, they are deadly. The listeners are more sought after. "People with the greatest social skills speak about as much as they listen," observes Majda Thurnher.

4. *Easing anxiety.* Philip Zimbardo, author of *Shyness*, says that the first step in improving social skills is to learn relaxation techniques. (We discussed some of those techniques in the previous chapter.) Often we are anxious about meeting new people and interacting with those we know already. A quiet time before a job interview, a party, or a meeting can work wonders. Worries about what people think tend to slip away, leaving you free to enjoy the encounter.

5. *Action*. Another basic rule is to *do something*. Once you do it, you will discover an untapped reservoir of energy that will get you through the encounter. Choose somebody who is sitting alone or on the edge of a group. Don't choose someone who is busy doing something else. Call out, "Hello! How are you?" Talk about your life, their life, the situation you are both in. If worse comes to worst, mention the weather.

   Small talk bores you? Think of it as a prelude to a more meaningful relationship. Sitting home alone will spare you the small talk but also the relationship. "But I already have good friends," you might say. "I don't need this." Remember Janet, the bridge player who had good friends. Where were they when she needed them? In the cemetery!

6. *Rehearse*. Think of yourself as an actor getting ready to go on stage. What will you say? Conversation that is planned is phony, but that doesn't mean you can't have a repertoire of interesting and funny happenings to relate if they seem to fit in. Read the newspaper, see the movies and plays in town, read the new books. A professional actor doesn't leave anything to chance before a performance, and neither should an emerging social butterfly.

7. *Concentrate on others, and respond*. Shy people are tuned in to their own uneasy feelings in a conversation. Socially skillful people observe others and are quick to react to their statements. They are quicker to affirm others by their attention and their remarks. They also direct their behavior to all members of a group evenly, not zeroing in on one person. A main difference here may be timing. While the shy person is anxiously sizing things up, the socially apt one is already reacting—not to inner thoughts but to what the person is saying. The cautious one eventually will react; but conversations move along

quickly, and by the time the shy person thinks of a response it may be too late.

8. *Speak up!* Women often have high, soft voices. This is a definite handicap. It's very possible to develop a deeper, fuller vocal tone. Learning to speak from the diaphragm and lower the voice can improve a woman's interaction with the world. A surprising number of the women I talked with have had training in public speaking through Toastmasters International. Consult your local telephone directory for information on Toastmasters International meetings in your community. The address of the national headquarters is given in Chapter 5.

9. *Speaking with power.* Women often apologize about everything—being a few minutes late, not knowing the answer to a question, not being some kind of an established expert on all subjects. They have been influenced to feel they are responsible for everything, so no wonder they feel they must apologize for any imperfection. Break yourself of this negative habit! Teach yourself to avoid remarks like, "It seems to me, but I may be wrong . . . " and "I know this is a stupid question, but. . . . " You'll be unable to convince your audience with whatever opinion follows.

If you have physically injured someone or broken a priceless Ming vase, apologize. Otherwise, don't! The apologies undermine your impact.

Group Skills

Majda Thurnher says, "It is most important for women to feel comfortable in groups. You don't have to be skilled in group interaction—just comfortable. This is harder when a woman gets older, especially if her self-esteem has gone down. It is not necessary to be at ease in all groups; not many people are. And it may be necessary to try many groups before finding the right one, just as you 'try out' many individuals before finding one good friend."

What benefits do groups bring? They are a source of friends and contacts and a source of emotional support and learning.

Support Groups   Clare Toth says, "Support groups that are centered around a common illness or circumstance often are more helpful to women than individual therapy."

Support groups are organized around almost every life situation and problem. There are groups for arthritis patients, Alzheimer's caretakers, people who have had cancer, and those who have tinnitus (ringing in the ears), phobias, or are widowed or newly divorced. Telephone your local information and referral agency, listed in the telephone directory. Some groups are started by community agencies, hospitals, churches, and therapists. It is also possible to start one of your own, using friends, church contacts, social agencies, or advertising in the local newspapers. A professional could lead the group to guide it, but that leader should not "have all the answers." Often we learn best from someone else who shares our concerns. Look for a group that goes beyond the sharing of sorrow to finding ways to grow. In a good group there is sharing of experiences, recognition of feelings, and learning about ways of coping. Groups could be formed to talk about the issues addressed in this book: What new horizons can women find when they are over fifty?

"We need to get women together who are fifty to seventy, and talk about our daily lives, concerns, and ideas for coping," Clare Toth believes. "Women need to accept themselves, deal with negative things that have happened as well as the positive, and learn to share themselves with others."

Special Interest Groups   Special interest and social groups also prevail in every community. After Sam died and Barbara moved to California, she found the Welcome Wagon group "a blessing." She has people to play bridge with, a book discussion group, evening parties to attend. Welcome Wagon contacts newcomers in a community. Membership can continue for three years. Although newcomers come in all ages, Welcome Wagon members tend to be homeowners over the age of forty. The group centers on couples; but Barbara joined anyway, and she found there also is a group of single people who do things together. One woman in Welcome Wagon said she recently moved to another house in the same community so she can extend her Welcome Wagon membership for three more years!

Churches are a good resource for finding out about special interest groups. One church in my area sponsors the Horizontal Hikers, a low-risk kind of hiking club.

Most newspapers list community activities. Photography, French, tennis, travel—there is no end to the kinds of organizations and clubs that are available. Enroll in a class at your local community college or parks and recreation department, YWCA, or Jewish Community Center. Are you interested in t'ai chi, writing, Mexican cooking, local history, dance, guitar, painting, sculpture? Don't be concerned about the ages of the other class members. Chances are there will be a few gray hairs—and anyway, it's fun to get to know people of all ages.

It's not important to be a group leader or to have special influence in the group. It *is* important to learn to be comfortable, be able to express yourself, and make some kind of social connections. If the first group you get in touch with doesn't hold your interest, try again! Contact at least four groups close together in time, making notes about what felt right or wrong with each. Then choose one or two to go back to.

Low-Cost Therapy Groups   Therapy groups are another important resource. Group therapy with a counselor puts you in touch with a therapist as well as a support group.

Most psychiatric hospitals schedule free lectures and workshops on family life, personal growth, and adjustment to difficult life situations. Social agencies do this, too, and often they present workshops. Watch the newspapers for announcements of these community programs.

There are community mental health agencies in every state that give counseling help regardless of ability to pay. Check your local information and referral agency.

Many books offer interesting ideas about living life more fully. Some of them are listed in the bibliography at the back of this book. Television talk shows are informative for many women. Oprah Winfrey, Phil Donahue, and Sally Jessy Raphael present provocative shows on women's issues. Many people listen and learn from radio therapists David Viscott and Toni Grant. Never has there been such an explosion of information—mostly free—on good mental health. "My space" and "reinforcement" are commonly understood terms. "Support" used to be an engineering term (as in a building or a bridge), or it implied financial help (as in child support). Now it is used to express that level of friendship and caring that unites us.

GOING BACK TO SCHOOL

Too old to go back to school and start a new career? Are you sure about that? All of the women I talked with who felt good about their lives had continued their education. Anna Cullinan and Kate Maxwell received scholarships and obtained graduate degrees. Dr. Grace Kaiser took graduate writing courses and attended writers' workshops. The classes gave her impetus and knowledge about the craft of writing and enabled her to make the change from physician to writer. Poet Doris Reed took adult education classes when she was in her seventies. She studied philosophy, Spanish, history, poetry, painting, and semantics. "Language is powerful," Doris says, "and education about its use has been enlightening."

Eileen's Story

Eileen Feuerbach is a slim, attractive woman from Virginia. At sixty-nine, she is now completing her doctoral thesis in clinical psychology at George Mason University.

Eileen had responded to the 1950s pressures to be a housewife and mother. Furthermore, she was a Navy wife, with special social and supportive obligations, who was required to move too often to establish her own career.

At fifty-five, Eileen felt there was something she wanted to do, in fact *needed* to do, and wasn't doing. An adult son was living at home, and her parents were senile and required care. Eileen realized that even though she was involved in all of their needs, she also needed to fulfill herself. She had enjoyed her housewife-mother role, but now she was finding it less satisfying. "If I had known how long it would go on," she said, "I would have made plans sooner for my life."

Eileen applied at the university. Losing her nerve, she had to fill out three application forms before she finally completed the process. The idea of returning to the classroom after all those years was terrifying. When one of her professors asked the class to write essays on their professional goals, Eileen realized she hadn't any. The professor encouraged her to determine a goal, telling her that she would be surprised how much her life experiences would help her to reach that goal. "This was music to my ears," she exclaimed.

Eileen enrolled in a doctoral program in psychology. She received a fellowship and a letter from the dean: "We are pleased to support bright young scholars like yourself." When the dean met her, he was in for quite a surprise!

Eileen's doctoral thesis explores the retirement of women, how they relate to it, and how satisfying they find it. She hopes to find employment in gerontology, a field that is less apt to discriminate against older women.

Many Educational Options

What is it like to be a student who is old enough to be the mother or grandmother of one's classmates? Sometimes it is difficult, since those younger students may be at a time in life when they want to get away from Mother. But many other students enjoy knowing alive, interesting older women. And most older women enjoy going back to school. They find people who are responsive to what they have to offer.

Because community colleges are less expensive than most four-year colleges, they are more likely to attract older students. However, age is no barrier to financial aid. Student loans and grants are not just for the young.

All universities and community colleges have adult education programs that offer low-cost and convenient ways to learn. The courses cover many cultural, philosophical, artistic, sometimes practical subjects, along with languages and physical education. They are not as demanding as the regular courses, require little or no homework, and meet only a few times a week. Many older men and women take advantage of these classes. No college credit is given, so classes are designed for the person looking for an avocation. However, many of the courses can be the basis for a career change or new life interest. They provide an excellent way to try out a new field before investing time and effort in a program leading to a degree.

Other organizations offer inexpensive classes. Local parks and recreation departments, for example, teach pottery, painting, Chinese cooking, and offer athletic activities. There are endless educational opportunities for adults. The libraries usually have course catalogs for all these resources.

Libraries themselves often have low-cost or free courses in creative writing, poetry, literature, and keeping a personal journal. Art museums, historical societies, and other community organizations also offer educational opportunities.

The metaphysical world offers courses in many cities. You can study meditation, spiritual healing, massage, how to develop psychic ability. Two years ago, Jane Turner, a former secretary, enrolled in a class to learn Kahuna, a Hawaiian method of developing insight and personal growth. She has studied dream interpretation, oriental healing methods, and how to expand her personality through visualization. At the workshops she has met friends of similar interests, all caring and enlightened people. These courses are plentiful in some cities. They are not listed in the newspaper or catalogs from the library, however. Inquire about them at the local massage school, metaphysical bookstore, or Unity church.

Elderhostel is another resource for growth. The older person may stay at a university in a foreign country for a few weeks, take lectures from a faculty member, and meet interesting people, all at can't-afford-to-stay-home prices.

Can You Teach an Old Dog New Tricks?

But how about the older brain—isn't it disintegrating? Not if we use it! Research on learning and aging is complex and the results are variable. There is evidence that older people do not do well on experimental tasks that are unrelated to their personal interests, whereas a younger person may enter into the task with spirit in the interest of "science." So older people are at a disadvantage in those tasks. Nevertheless, there is ample research to show that people can learn in their later years, although at a slower pace and preferably with tasks that are meaningful to them.

Many people fear going back to school because they forget where they put the car keys. "If I can't remember a simple thing like that, I'll never be able to learn a history course," they fear. This is unfortunate, because there are different kinds of memory involved in each task. A study at the National Institute on Aging found that there is a decline in "visual-spatial" memory, the ability to recall spatial relationships. This is the car key phenomenon. The kind of memory required for learning in the classroom is different, and one that we do not lose to the extent we might fear. Furthermore, most course work involves writing, which provides a way of keeping the mind flowing without having to do much memorizing. Older people require more time to retrieve information, but it does come. One woman said, "I know that fact. I can't think of it now, but I will because I still know it." This is a healthy attitude because it respects the basic ability of the brain to retain knowledge. This relaxed frame of mind is conducive to the recall.

Mental abilities can continue all through life, but we do need to practice. Mental activity exercises the brain. Remembering items in one area seems to stimulate remembering in others.

In his book, *How to Improve Your Memory,* James D. Weinland describes some exercises to get the brain back in shape. He asks you to combine visual imagery with the fact or thought you want to remember. For instance, you want to remember to mail a letter in the mailbox in a downtown office. Visualize yourself going to the mailbox and dropping the letter through the slot. Do it with concentration. Repeat the visualization several times. Repetition, visualization, and the intention to remember are all effective memory techniques. Persons who remember the best have the attitude of an explorer. They find interesting things to learn and have an emotional investment in learning.

Some people claim that playing bridge has kept their memory in good shape.

For those who have severe memory problems, a medical checkup is indicated. Some physical conditions and medications may interfere with memory. Other people—or worse, the person himself—may think he is senile when he has a physical problem that can be treated.

A VOLUNTEER CAREER

To be involved in the community on a long-term basis, try volunteering. The days are past when volunteer work meant rolling bandages and stuffing envelopes. Now it can be challenging enough to be called a career. My Sunday newspaper lists enough of these opportunities to make a good choice. The local branch of a national institution would like someone to work on children's programs. A crisis hot line at a psychiatric hospital can use a counselor. The public television station needs people to monitor audiovisual material and help with live productions. A mental health agency wants a part-time office manager and another person who will interview Spanish-speaking families. A center for abused children asks for someone to answer the telephone. The art museum on the university campus is forming docent classes. After learning art history and theory and sharpening their communication skills, the volunteers will lead groups through the museum and explain each painting or sculpture. The zoo also is looking for volunteers to conduct tours for school groups. A clinic wants volunteer physicians. Any of these openings could form the nucleus for a life's purpose.

SCORE, sponsored by the federal Small Business Administration, is a group of retired business people who give free counseling to others who are planning to start new businesses. There is always a need for more participants with specialized knowledge.

The benefits are mutual. The volunteer receives some of the amenities he or she had at work—a telephone, a place to hold meetings, educational programs, guidance, and—happy day!—colleagues. The greatest benefit is that the work provides an outlet for the creativity and perspective of middle age to be expressed.

If you want to be the most valuable person in town, join the volunteer staff of a telephone crisis line. These volunteers save lives every day, deterring people from suicide, getting help to those with specific needs, and providing emotional support. Crisis centers offer extensive training in a type of counseling called "crisis intervention." Volunteers are taught how to relate quickly to a caller, how to listen effectively, and how to respond in a way that enables the caller to go forward. This course is so good that professional counselors sometimes take it as a supplement to their regular courses. After the training, volunteers are scheduled to answer calls regularly, usually about four hours a week plus some overnights. A supervisor is always there as well.

Consider designing your own volunteer program, based on a community need that you see. The volunteer center in your community can help you find an agency that would like to work with you. If you don't see the volunteer center in the telephone book or newspaper, call the local information and referral number.

When volunteering for a professional type of job, you may be asked to present a resume. Agencies need to maintain a professional level of service, whether or not they provide a paycheck.

ACTIVISM

Working toward righting the wrongs of society is difficult, to say the least; but many people find that the effort makes their lives more meaningful. Working for change also offers an outlet for the anger that often results from the experience of being a woman in our culture. What could be more constructive for women than to actively protest the status quo by working with agencies that are promoting change? Poverty has become a women's issue, with 75 percent of the poor being women and children. Community agencies do much to help, but these agencies usually evolved from the initial efforts of people with a pioneering spirit—volunteers. The Gray Panthers, for example, concentrate their efforts on obtaining better housing for older people. They also work on medical care issues. The Older Women's League is working on the issue of age discrimination in employment. For further information, write to 730 11th St. N.W., Suite 300, Washington, D.C. 20001.

Peace is another issue that is close to the hearts of women. Several women I talked with give their time to the Women's International League for Peace and Freedom. Women know how much work and commitment goes into the growth of a single human being, and many of those women are enraged by war.

VOCATIONAL GUIDANCE

"I am ready for something different in my life, but I don't know what it is." This seems to be the cry of many women over fifty. They have education, talent, a varied life experience—but now what? They flounder in confusion and frustration.

Vocational counseling has enabled many women to get started in a new direction. But other women complain that vocational guidance is designed for younger women. They feel that counselors don't always take into account the older woman's experience and special difficulties in the labor market. The services also fail to look at life itself as a career. Not everyone wants a paid job at sixty, but many people do want some kind of guidance about what their life path should be. Should they take up the violin? Retire to a community where golf is important? Live by a lake in Vermont and study fish? With the last third of life at hand, it is all the more urgent to make good decisions about life goals and purposes. Consultation with a career counselor can be invaluable.

A Model Program

Options for Women Over Forty is a comprehensive program instituted by the University of San Francisco. The program provides counseling, testing for aptitudes and interests, and preparation for the job market or aid in setting goals for some other meaningful activity. The organization has offered assessment for employment, support groups, and crisis work since its opening in 1978, and counseling services became available in July 1988. The agency serves all women over forty on a sliding fee scale. This means that an "advantaged" woman can benefit and pay a low fee, or a "disadvantaged" woman can go and pay no fee. Since an advantaged woman can quickly become disadvantaged with the loss of a husband, she needs such a program.

Counselor Joan Visser was trained in life transitions counseling at the University of San Francisco. This type of counseling focuses on the process of life transitions. Joan views her job as having four goals:

1. Assisting women in grieving over the past and learning to let go of their pain.
2. Helping women to look into the past to find talents and interests that can be brought into the present, and then counseling women about how those talents can be utilized in the work world.
3. Giving personality and aptitude tests to further assist in setting employment goals.
4. Preparing women for the work world, training them in preparing a resume and interviewing for a job.

Career Counseling for the Displaced Homemaker

"Women are in a more vulnerable position than they realize," says Diane Wilson, a counselor at a community program for "displaced homemakers" in Arizona.

The woman who has devoted her life to home, husband, and family is at risk when she loses him through divorce or death. Diane describes these women's situation as desperate. Usually they are too old for Aid to Dependent Children, too young for Social Security, and they are unable to find work.

Most of the women Diane meets in her work have been turned down at job interviews and employment agencies. They feel personally rejected. Restoring self-esteem is the first priority in Diane's program. Every applicant goes through an intake, orientation, and career-testing process, all designed to increase self-esteem. On the first day, women are asked to express their needs, and then to describe what they might have to offer to an employer. Just beginning to talk about themselves as a potential employee allows them to see themselves in a new way. They also give one another mutual support. They learn that they are not alone. On the second day, the support group meets for two hours. The group continues to meet once a week.

Once a month there is a two-week job search workshop, which helps the participants to identify areas they might want to look into for training or employment. They are taught how to go about the search. They learn how to write a resume, how to interview, and how to talk about themselves in positive ways. Employers come in to talk to them about the qualities they seek in applicants, and the clients learn to recognize and develop those qualities in themselves.

COMMUNITY SERVICES

Most communities have an information and referral agency listed in the telephone directory. There you can learn about local agencies that give comprehensive services to women.

There are many governmental and community agencies for the older person, such as the local council on aging. A close look indicates that "aging" means *old*—not the younger, fifty-plus women. Government grants to this council now focus on housing and nutrition needs of the elderly, physical and behavioral problems, Alzheimer's disease, and research about the process of aging itself. But the late middle-agers are another group entirely. The council can put them in touch with community services to help with an aging parent who might need care, however. That kind of help then would free the fifty-year-old woman to pursue her own interests.

Community agencies can help by focusing on common human needs that are shared by those in their fifties or sixties. Legal aid societies and state-sponsored mental health centers are available. Societies for the hard of hearing touch on problems that are relevant to that group. Family Service and Catholic Social Services work with people and families of all ages. These and similar social agencies have information about all resources in your community.

County health departments can refer you to programs for middle-aged men and women who are taking care of older persons. They offer assistance to the families and sponsor educational programs and caregivers' support groups. They also assist in placing older or handicapped family members in nursing homes, if needed.

Volunteer community organizations are available to help women deal with specific problems that are more apt to happen in late middle age. There are groups to counsel retired or divorced officers' wives. The National Organization for Women (NOW) works on *all* women's issues. Retirement planning centers offer financial planning, dealing with the special concerns of the older age group that are not always well met by conventional financial organizations. These planning centers also provide community education on retirement, and usually they have a small library of books on the health and psychological needs of people who are getting ready to retire.

The Alzheimer's Association provides education and support groups for families. "You thought these would be the golden years?" asked the group leader at one meeting. "They are hell!" His comments paved the way for a lot of mutual sharing among those who had the care of a parent or spouse with Alzheimer's disease. Group members are kept up-to-date on the latest research, medicines, and resources for help.

The American Parkinson's Disease Association performs a similar service. Cancer societies hold educational and support meetings for patients and families, as does the Arthritis Foundation. There is a National Foundation for Ileitis and Colitis, two difficult-to-live-with diseases of the bowels. The

Lupus Foundation of America holds meetings in many communities. Other organizations help people who have had strokes. The Alliance for the Mentally Ill serves as an advocate for the long-term mentally ill, giving support and educational services to the family.

There are organizations to help people lose weight, stop smoking, overcome alcoholism, meet other single people of their age. Every community has a resource catalog of services available to social-work professionals. These can be located with a few telephone calls to agencies. Local newspapers often publish lists of meetings.

Despite the vast amount of community education and support, programs that meet the unique needs of late middle-agers would be a welcome addition. Often the problem is not in coping with a specific illness, but in finding new horizons and people with whom to share the search.

RECREATION

Most older people enjoy increased leisure, finally reading the books they always wanted to read as well as the new ones. Each book can open the mind to a whole new world. Some people join a book group, others enjoy their privacy and their reading.

Many people find that tennis or golf or swimming becomes their new life. A multimillion-dollar industry is built around the new retirees who have energy and money and like sports. Retirement and leisure villages provide them a safe place to live, often in a beautiful location, away from the turmoil of the regular world and close to golf courses, tennis courts, and swimming pools. For those who enjoy the recreational and social life with others in the same age group who share the same interests, these communities can be paradise.

But for the person who doesn't share those interests, who doesn't like bridge or golf or endless parties, these communities can be a trap. They are usually located away from the general community, so it is difficult to be "different"—to try Kahuna training or volunteer to help at the hospice center or start a new business. If you are thinking of moving to this kind of community, you would be wise to spend some time there to be sure it is the right lifestyle for you. Will it still be the right path if you are widowed? Are single women left out of things? Or do they have an active round of activities themselves? Are there cliques? Look into these communities very carefully before you leap!

For those who stay in the city or the suburbs, there are public and private golf courses, courts, and pools—especially in the Sun Belt centers of the country. So it is possible to have it all—enjoy the recreational activities of a community and do other things, too.

ADVENTURE

Curiosity and a fascination with the world are great qualities for successful aging. Travel—whether in organized groups, Elderhostel trips, or independent adventure—is exciting and stimulating. Exploring, camping, learning about the history and wildlife of your area, is a reaching out that enriches many people's lives. I know a retired couple in their fifties who conduct study groups for the Audubon Society and take people to nearby canyons on bird-watching tours. For this couple, it is a fulfilling new adventure that is close to home.

Those who are limited by illness need creative opportunities for adventure. A friend whose lung cancer causes much shortness of breath misses her hikes in the woods. The last time she went with friends, she had to lag behind and return alone. She is organizing a slower hiking group, which she believes will be just as exciting though not as demanding. (Remember the tortoise and the hare!)

Many seniors lead groups to finance their desire for travel. Recently I met two retired musicians who were leading a music-oriented tour of Europe. A friend, a former archaeology professor, arranges and leads tours of ancient Mayan ruins in the Yucatan. Thousands of older people travel in groups or independently. They are amazing in their enthusiasm for adventure. They climb up steep hills despite age and aching muscles; they ride down perilous canyons on the backs of donkeys. Nothing seems to stop the person who is determined to see the world!

Gay Frank's New Horizons

On Gay Frank's sixtieth birthday she was in Saigon, leading a group of tourists through Southeast Asia. "It was nice to be somewhere exotic," she told me, "instead of sitting at home watching the wrinkles develop."

Gay has led groups on six-week trips to the Himalayan mountains, Africa, Burma, Borneo, Bali, Singapore, Malaysia, Thailand—all over the world. Gay spends a year arranging each trip, contacting participants, and planning unique experiences. Although the trips are expensive, they are not the kinds of adventures people could have on their own for less money—or, in fact, have at all. For instance, one year Gay took a group to Rwanda, in Africa, to see mountain gorillas in their native habitat. The tourists climbed a volcano to reach the cloud forest where those gigantic, incredible creatures live. There were no trails— just underbrush. Gay's partner is a world-famous naturalist who speaks many languages. Gay herself has become a naturalist. She has successfully combined her talent for organization and her ability to communicate effectively with her unbridled enthusiasm about the world and a sparkling sense of adventure!

How Gay Found Her New Horizons Gay grew up reading an encyclopedia called *The Book of Knowledge*. The books were filled with stories and pictures of old castles and exciting places. She always had a yen for adventure, and she was able to travel as a part of her college education. She obtained a degree in social work and worked for a child welfare agency until her marriage.

As a wife and mother, she stayed at home with the children—except that she was seldom technically "at home." She took the children to puppet shows, hikes, and picnics, went sledding in the winter, swimming in the summer, and picking apples in the fall. On their acre of land, they had forty-four animals—otters, armadillos, golden pheasants, bunnies, ducks, and a lame goose. When the children reached school age Gay drove them to school, then stayed to teach a French class.

After the children grew up, Gay wanted to do something very different from either social work or teaching French. She looked back at her childhood to find some clues to the right new career. Gay recalled that she had loved toads and robin eggs, and she loved to be outside. She plunged into natural history. Through her new knowledge, she developed a keen desire to see the rare animals she was reading about. While attending classes at the university as a student of natural history, she met her travel partner and they decided to join forces.

Too Old for Adventure? "Who goes on these exotic and strenuous trips?" I asked Gay. (I was visualizing husky football players and eighteen-year-old mountain climbers.) "Women in their fifties!" she replied. Although men and women of all ages have taken trips with Gay, the travelers generally are in their late forties through middle sixties, with the largest numbers in the mid-fifties. The women often traveled without their husbands.

You can be sure you're not going to be able to climb a volcano in Rwanda if you've spent the year walking from your living room to the carport and back! What does Gay do to keep in shape in between trips? Although many people run, lift weights, and exercise in other ways, Gay believes that the people who do best are those who climb stairs. At home, she has an exercise machine that simulates the stairs, as well as a machine that simulates cross-country skiing.

Gay started her crucial fiftieth decade by going to Outward Bound, a supervised program of rigorous physical adventure. (Again I had a vision of the people who enroll in that program: eighteen-year-old daredevils!) Gay says, "They would rather see people like us come in than they would young people in the peak of their form, who are already confident. The whole idea of the program is to build up your confidence by pushing yourself to extremes that you never dreamed were possible. The exhilaration that follows is overwhelming ('My God! I did that!'), and the thrill and self-confidence remain. You don't have to go around rappeling down cliffs for the rest of your life, but you do take on jobs or challenges that otherwise you would have thought were beyond your abilities—and not all in the physical area."

If these trips sound irresistible, you may be too late to go with Gay; she is thinking about moving on to new challenges. She does want to go on one more trip to New Guinea to see the bowerbird, a tiny bird that weaves a shelter of vines for its mate and each day redecorates the nest with fresh flowers; and to Northern Australia, where the aborigines still live a fairly pure existence. Gay's excitement over this next adventure affirms the secret of her success: curiosity, zest for life, and a deep sense that the world is indeed a fascinating place!

CHAPTER SEVEN

Older Women in the Business World

The trim, neatly dressed woman looks across the desk at her interviewer, a young man who is about the age of her youngest son. The interviewer has been carefully selected by management to convey "the right image" that represents the upbeat, growing nature of the organization. This bright, energetic young executive looks on the older interviewee with some skepticism. "She looks like my mother," crosses his mind. The well-educated older woman may be a threat in other ways. "Ph.D.," he reads on the application form. "I don't have that myself. She may end up taking my job." The interviewer wonders if the applicant can adapt to the way things are done in the organization. "She may be set in her ways." Interviewers quickly size up an applicant's ability to fit in. "How would it be to work with her?" Not surprisingly, the answer is usually, "risky." The applicant is told she has no valid experience; or, if she has had years of experience, "You are overqualified." Either way, she is turned down for the job.

Work fulfills many needs, income not the least of them. It provides social cooperation and interaction, a life goal, and recognition. Unfortunately, many women over fifty are employed below the level of their training and abilities or are not employed at all. The unchallenging job is the more frustrating. The woman without 9-to-5 commitments is free to pursue other meaningful activities; but the woman who must work, or wants to work for the psychological benefits it brings, is in for a struggle.

Counselor Diane Wilson says, "When a woman reenters the job market, the level of employment that she finds probably will be the level at which she will remain. It is not possible for an older employee to start out as errand girl with hopes of rising to be an executive secretary. It is necessary to get the training first." Women with limited education who want to work, or who need to work after a divorce or widowhood, have little choice but to take low-level jobs that have no future. If no money problems are anticipated in case of widowhood or divorce, a wife still has the advantage of exploring her interests while she has financial support at home.

Fortunate is the woman who has developed employable skills along the way, who has kept up with her professional connections, is employed at a job she enjoys, and has retained her health. The average age for a woman to become widowed is fifty-six. Many women are provided for by their husbands, but not all are. Divorce, chronic illnesses, economic downturns can change financial situations quickly and drastically. Several of the women I talked with who had money as inheritance or divorce settlements saw their investments dwindle in the stock market crash in 1987. Overnight, they became as vulnerable as the women who had not had money.

YOUNGER WORKERS PREFERRED

The main obstacle to finding work, according to the National Commission on Working Women, is that employers prefer younger workers. The commission published a report outlining the major problems. What is not generally recognized is the fact that these problems exist regardless of a woman's education and employment record. A highly skilled professional has the same problems in this regard as the displaced homemaker with rusty skills and little or no experience in the job market.

1. *Inverse sexual discrimination.* A woman without physical beauty and youth is often considered unemployable. Women are considered "old" at an early age, usually about forty.

   The Equal Employment Opportunity Commission cites the preferences of male executives for attractive young women on their staffs. This practice occurs in business and government alike. Older women may be pressured to retire. One woman was transferred to a back office at the age of sixty-two because she "no longer fit in." She had worked for the company for nineteen years and had an excellent work record. After the demotion, her self-esteem dropped rapidly.

2. *Ageism.* A well-qualified fifty-five-year-old applicant may be told that she "doesn't fit our image." This usually means that the employees all are under the age of thirty. Many companies recruit mainly from college campuses, thereby ensuring a youthful work force.

   Virtually every woman over forty who has an

education and job experience has been told that she is "overqualified" for a job. One woman dropped most of her credentials from her resume, and still she was told she was overqualified. Women tell me they have learned to decipher words used in want ads. "Bright, energetic" is a code word for young. "Mature" means the job doesn't pay much. After the interview, "overqualified" means old.

In some ways, educated women are more penalized by ageism. Their professional work is more meaningful to them, and the lack of it more frustrating.

3. *Economic realities.* Employers are faced with increasing medical insurance costs. Older employees cost them higher insurance rates. Employers also fear a rise in their workmen's compensation insurance bill if they hire older workers. The chances of an older worker becoming disabled are seen as greater. The years close to retirement are especially risky for the woman worker. Her chances for pay raises are lowered, thus limiting her pension.

4. *The new "marginalization" of the work force.* We hear about mergers, reorganizations, and "cutting down to the bone." What we don't hear is that the "waste" that is eliminated is most apt to be the older employees. Employers are increasing their use of part-time and temporary employees. In *9 to 5*, published by the National Association of Working Women, we read that "older workers are the 'shock absorbers' for the changing economy." These marginal workers have low pay, few benefits, and no job security. Older workers are the most likely to be hurt by layoffs and are most apt to be used as short-term workers to cut down expenses.

Many companies now rehire retired employees. This sounds like progress until you realize that the pay is now lower, even though the worker may bring long years of experience, and the pension and benefit package suffers. Older women with job tenure suffer the greatest loss of earnings when rehired.

"But they want to work part-time," employers insist. The Older Women's League, in a 1989 report, says there is evidence to the contrary. Often they have no choice. Younger women might take heed while they still have options. After a certain age, a woman finds that "part time employment is a time bomb ticking in her economic future."

And so women who have jobs hold on to them, realizing that there aren't many other jobs out there. This creates a pressure to conform, no matter how negative the work environment. These women experience anxiety about their job tenure. The anxiety may make them defensive and uncertain at times, and their employers may view them as being "difficult."

Anita Romero notes the vast difference in goals between the younger and older employees she works with. The younger women talk about career advancement, raises, and training opportunities. The older women, who are seldom invited to the training programs, talk about retirement and seem discouraged about their jobs. Hispanic women face a double stress. They return home after work to their old jobs. Husbands and other relatives cling to the idea that the home is the wife's responsibility, and she is judged solely on that criterion—how often the rug is vacuumed, how elaborate her meals are. Never mind that she is also earning a living for the family.

The Next Bag Lady You See

"The next bag lady you see," says Diane Wilson, "is a woman who could have been helped with employment issues somewhere along the line." Women over sixty-five are the fastest growing poverty group in the country. The discrimination that plagued them all along now translates into no pension plan, even though they have worked all their lives—in the home and out. Only 20 percent of retirement-aged women receive pensions, and those pensions tend to be unlivably low. The majority of older women can no longer depend on a husband's income. No wonder that the women who come to displaced homemakers' agencies are desperate!

A Note About "Little Old Ladies"

Do short women with gray hair have the hardest time? Caroline, the housewife turned journalist, thinks so as she sees women of that description patted condescendingly on the head. Caroline is over sixty too, but she is tall and tints her hair. One person saying it doesn't make it so; yet it may be worth noting. Society does have a bias against age, shortness, and women, and the three out of three may be too much. Caroline compensates with the tint, and an authoritative manner.

Blaming the Victim

Today women have a multitude of choices about their life's work and a lot of support about those choices. It is easy for them to jump to the conclusion that the older women they know "should have" done the same. In that time warp we call the 1950s, it wasn't that clear to most women that they had real choices. Education for women was available, but not the opportunities or the encouragement. Birth control was not as effective, and women were made to feel guilty about using it. Society sent a strong message to women that raising children was their true vocation.

Raising children is important, and there is a sad irony in the present belief that a woman who stays home "isn't doing anything." When homemakers do seek another career at age forty, fifty, sixty, seventy, they deserve encouragement, not, "Well, you should have done that before" or, from prospective employers, "You are overqualified for this job."

Who Is Vulnerable? Isabelle's Story

Isabelle was married to Carl, a successful design engineer. They had a large home in a New York suburb, two cars in the garage, and three children. Carl's job was eliminated in a business recession. After many months, he was hired by an oil firm, and he and Isabelle moved to Texas. Once settled in Houston and with time on her hands, Isabelle decided to take some training in computer skills. While in training, she took a part-time job in data entry, working at minimum wage. The oil company went bankrupt, and Carl, being newly hired, was the first to go.

Isabelle remained in school and kept on working, but she wasn't earning enough money to pay their bills. They lost their home, their furniture, their savings. Finally they had nothing more to sell, and they cashed in Carl's life insurance policy. A year later, Carl died of a heart attack. There was no money to pay his funeral expenses.

When Isabelle came to the displaced homemakers' agency, she was desperate for some kind of income, right away. She had no time left to pursue additional training. Diane Wilson helped her find a job immediately. The job is part-time, offers no benefits, but does pay more than minimum wage. So far, the agency has not been able to arrange for any kind of permanent job with benefits for her.

Isabelle is now fifty-six years old. She is intelligent and warm, and she has a college degree and computer training; yet she is in a panic about how she is going to survive in a workplace that resists hiring women her age. She is in a better situation, but still not in a secure place. She has no retirement benefits, no health benefits, and no assurance that her job will be ongoing.

College Is Not an Insurance

I was surprised to learn from Diane Wilson that a college degree over twenty years old tends to be discounted. About 10 to 12 percent of the women coming to the counseling center have college degrees. If they followed up the degree with at least ten years of work experience in their field, they have a better chance of getting a job. But many of those women married right after college and stayed home to raise their families.

No-Fault Divorce

The new no-fault divorce means that men can leave with their future earnings intact, but the woman usually has to begin anew. Courts are unwilling to award spousal maintenance. After a long-term marriage, the wife can work through a lawyer to get a better settlement; but if the divorce goes through the court system, she has very little chance of getting alimony. The courts will award child support until age eighteen. If a woman can get spousal maintenance for two years, she can take the opportunity to go to school for career training and can enter the labor market at a higher level. Today's women are usually smart enough to come to a counseling agency and begin working on the problem right away, not wait until the two years' support is gone.

Smarter yet would be the woman who starts working on this problem when the marriage shows signs of fraying or the husband first becomes ill. Low-income women are eligible for displaced homemakers' programs even if they are married and their husbands are employed.

DISCRIMINATION AND THE LAW

But isn't discrimination against the law? Yes, it is, and that is why age discrimination has to be so subtle. It is a "hidden discrimination." It is all the harder to fight, because employers do not recognize it as existing. "You're over-qualified" and "We hired someone with more training," the job applicant hears. It is difficult for the job applicant to know if the rejection is discrimination or not. She doesn't see the other applicants or read their resumes. In government agencies, where records are made public, a clear case of discrimination is easier to spot.

A confidential interview with a woman who works in affirmative action for a large government agency indicates that even in that working place there is a problem. Cathy Morrison is glowing with energy, health, and youthful enthusiasm at forty-five. People come to her with racial discrimination claims, complaints about age bias, and other problems in the agency. Cathy's job is to resolve complaints so they needn't reach the higher agencies that explore discrimination. If someone has a difficulty with management, she sits down with everyone concerned and mediates the discussion. But Cathy says that once the immediate problem is solved, management glosses over the underlying causes, and later the problem comes right back. Cathy says that making a formal complaint, with all the difficulties involved, is the only permanent solution. Yet her job is to prevent complaints from being taken to a higher force. It frustrates her that while she is working for the benefit of the employees, she is at the same time working against their interests by smoothing things over.

Cathy talked to personnel at the higher investigatory agency to ask about age discrimination claims. She was told that a lot of them are investigated, but that the complaints are mainly "trivial." An older worker may complain about not getting his choice of a vacation time when younger workers are given their choices. Another says she was not given the job development training that younger workers were given. The agency personnel representatives who hear these complaints tend to dismiss them as inaccurate or unnecessary. Cathy says this is an alarming trend. She sees it as denial that age discrimination does exist. Women are especially vulnerable by being less assertive and less skilled in waging a successful battle for their rights. It is important for all employees to know their rights. The government has specific procedures, but people in the private sector are less apt to be informed about their rights and how to enforce them.

It *is* possible to challenge employers. In the private sector, the state Attorney General's office, Civil Rights Division, investigates age discrimination cases. Legal action may hamper a woman's effectiveness to work for that organization, but often the woman is being overlooked already or is being given poor references.

SO NOW WHAT DO WE DO?

Frustrating though the search may be, women over fifty often do find suitable employment. Usually they need to work harder to find those jobs than do younger women, and they need to look for good employment advice. Despite this negative picture, the main ingredient in success is to think positively!

Ten Things to Do as You Begin the Job Search

1. It is important to retain positive feelings about yourself and your optimism, while at the same time taking a

realistic look at your options. This may seem to be a contradictory balancing act; yet both attitudes are essential.

2. Realize the extent to which society contributes to this difficult situation. The endless rejections are not your fault.

3. Society may say that you are too old for good jobs, but if you accept this verdict you are done before you start.

4. Upgrade your education when possible. Realize that even if you have an M.B.A., it won't help much if it was conferred thirty years ago and wasn't followed by employment. Even if you have a long but interrupted history of work, the last five years had better contain some work-related activity and a refresher course in your business or profession.

5. Assess your skills and interests, and determine exactly what you have to contribute to the job market. We tend to discredit the executive ability that is required to run a home successfully. As homemakers, women finely hone their skills in marketing, time management, and dealing with difficult people, along with a host of other marketable skills.

6. Assess the market. Talk with personnel counselors in the employment offices of hospitals, businesses, and other places where you might want to work. Find out which positions they have a hard time filling. A good employment counselor can help you match your skills with the needs of the marketplace.

7. Don't defeat yourself with false ideas about aging. It's enough that employers have them. Have you ever heard, "If you haven't made it by age forty, you never will?" If you believe this, you *certainly* never will!

8. Yes, you can learn to use a computer! Many older people decide they just can't adjust to all the new methods in the business world. *You can!* And you can

learn the current professional jargon. Words like "systems approach" and "logistics" are nothing more than new names for concepts you already know by other names.

Anita Romero notices that when employers give training in the new methods to all employees, the older workers seem to ask a lot of questions. The questions come from anxiety, and they may lead the supervisors to think the older workers can't learn. What those employees don't realize is that the younger workers don't understand the changes either, but they figure them out as they go along. Remember that it isn't age but anxiety that you may be "too old to learn" that is causing the problem. Let this knowledge help you to relax and learn the new ways.

9. After a discouraging job search, avoid thinking, "It doesn't matter anyway; this is the end of the line. I might as well stay home and relax." If you want a job enough to look for one, the job must represent an important need in your life. Go for it!

10. Get training in how to write a resume and how to present yourself in a job interview.

How to Interview to Beat the Age Bias

Don't think the employer doesn't notice that you are older than other applicants. Instead of ignoring age, Diane Wilson suggests that women over fifty confront the issue, gently bringing up the unspoken concerns in the conversation. "You will know from my resume that I have had years of experience." (*Not* "I am older.") Employers are concerned about workers getting along with each other. "I have experience in getting along with a variety of people over the years," you might point out. "I am very committed to the work ethic. I am reliable and dependable."

Employers already know that older workers tend to be the most reliable and hard-working employees. They know that maturity has given those older workers skills in settling conflict. And they know that younger workers tend to be more restless and may not be willing to devote all their energies to the job. They also may be less inclined to work with people they disagree with. Prospective employers know these facts; but it doesn't hurt to remind them of the many benefits they gain by hiring mature workers.

How Relevant Is Your Volunteer Work?

Employers are beginning to consider the merits of a job applicant's volunteer work. There is one catch, however. Be sure that your recent volunteer work includes some work that is relevant to your professional skills. For instance, if you are a social worker by education and now you are a volunteer guide at the local zoo, this may not count. But if you get involved in training and organizing volunteers at the zoo, it will. On the other hand, a teacher will find that being a docent calls forth her teaching skills, so her volunteer experience will be considered relevant by an employer. If you have other skills that have nothing to do with the kind of job you want, it might be just as well to keep them off the resume. See a vocational counselor for specific advice.

Where Are the Jobs?

By researching the answer to this complicated question, you'll avoid a lot of the demoralizing stress of fruitless job hunting. Since 80 percent of jobs are found through contacts, a first step might be to renew old professional contacts and make new ones; in other words, "network." Women often dislike "using" their friends in this way; yet this is how people hear about existing and expected job openings, and it's how potential employers hear about available workers.

Consider which skills are in demand. Clerical positions are usually available in most areas. Women who have had experience volunteering in the community may find that they have the skills and experience to run a community organization, a social agency, or a nonprofit institution such as a clinic. Real estate is another popular field for women, who have a natural ability to size up a house in terms of its prospective owners. Some of the most successful women in real estate started in midlife.

Women have personal knowledge of family concerns. No wonder they make good financial planners, insurance sales personnel, and travel agents. Retail clothing stores employ many middle-aged women as buyers and salespeople.

Health service is a rapidly expanding field. A hospital employment officer says that technical skills that hospitals use are always in demand. Find out which skills are needed, what training is required, and where to get it.

Technical training in the health field has the advantage of not taking years to acquire. Some skills can be learned in less than a year. Another major advantage is that the skill is immediately marketable, whereas a university program leading to a degree might be speculative.

Getting Career Counseling

Women who have been out of the job market for years need reorientation. It's a tall order—to evaluate skills that were used in the home or in volunteer activities, determine personal aptitudes, and figure out how to translate this into today's job market.

A search for the ideal kind of agency led me to Washington, D.C., where many career counseling services exist. A number of them are for the "disadvantaged woman," one who is without financial backing. I called one such agency to inquire about services that would help a woman of sixty find employment. After a brief silence, the woman at the agency replied, "We concentrate on career." I said, "I *mean* a career." She didn't respond, apparently feeling that no one could be thinking of a career at that age!

Telephone calls to whatever career counseling exists in one's area—universities and community colleges, the local psychological association—may bring forth some resources. For the woman doing it on her own, *Success Over Sixty*, a book written by Albert Myers and Christopher Anderson, can help the woman evaluate her skills and express them in language that business people understand. (For example, shopping for the family's many needs becomes "purchasing.") Another book, *What Color Is Your Parachute?*, by R.N. Bolles, offers practical methods to evaluate aptitudes and think creatively about a new direction.

But these books alone cannot help you match your knowledge with the job possibilities in a given community. An appointment with a counselor at an employment agency will get you started. Telephone calls to the many businesses and offices that are under consideration can provide the rest.

Starting Your Own Business

On the other hand, why wait for someone else to "allow" you to use your skills? Many men and women over fifty choose to go in business for themselves. Their experiences and their "common sense" approach to the world make them good entrepreneurs. Three of every five new businesses are started by women over fifty.

Inspiration and original ideas can help create a business that succeeds. But before making an investment in time and money, some realistic assessment has to take place. What is the market for your proposed service or product? What are your assets in providing it, and what are the potential problems?

Being your own boss is a natural for a person who is trained in a professional service. A counselor, physician, lawyer, accountant, writer, chef, all can start an independent practice with minimum financial investment. You do have to count the many months or years it takes to build a practice, however; so you must be sure that your particular service is needed, and you must have some kind of financial backing.

Many women enjoy selling a product that interests them, and they open art galleries, bookstores, dress shops, stationery stores, gourmet shops. For retail sales and restaurants, the financial risks are greater.

Small businesses are now a large part of the economy and account for 38 percent of all sales in this country. They are a popular way for people to extend their working years and have the experience of being their own boss. But there are also risks to a small business, and half of them fail in the first four years.

Motivation and ability aren't enough. Good business planning can make the difference between success and failure. A unique program comes to the rescue! The U.S. Small Business Administration provides the Service Corps Of Retired Executives (SCORE). These retired businessmen and women offer the benefit of their own successful experience. They volunteer their time, and there is no charge for their service. There have been Cinderella stories of businesses that with SCORE's help have grown to employ hundreds of people. There are more than 750 SCORE counseling agencies located in all fifty states, Puerto Rico, and Guam. You can find the nearest chapter by checking the telephone directory under the U.S. Small Business Administration, or by calling the toll-free hot line, 1-800-368-5855.

The fact that small businesses sometimes fail in itself is

not a deterrent. The problem is the financial risk, which is not welcome at this time of life. On the other hand, a well-planned enterprise, with a minimum risk, satisfies that important need to be in control of one's life. An owner of a successful business can hire other workers so business can continue if the owner wants to cut back on working hours and have more flexibility.

The revolution is coming! Baby boomers have not kept the population rate going. The law of supply and demand is beginning to work in favor of the worker over fifty. In some parts of the country where the supply of twenty-year-old workers is particularly short, businesses already are beginning to solicit older workers. The woman over fifty who can keep up her confidence and her skills will have new opportunities in the nineties.

THE PRICE OF "MAKING IT":
MIRIAM'S STORY

Miriam Haskell, a fiery sixty-eight-year-old judge in the Superior Court in her western city, is enthusiastic about her work. Currently she presides in the domestic court. Previously she worked in the juvenile court and she has sat on the civil and criminal benches. Miriam believes that her wide range of experiences allows her to make a significant contribution to the lives of women and children in her community.

What was it like for her to start a career in an era when women kept a low profile? Difficult! As a young undergraduate, Miriam enrolled in the premed program. At that time—the 1940s—the university didn't have a medical school, but she hoped to go to a medical school elsewhere. World War II intervened. Miriam got a job in a laboratory and married a young soldier who had been a dental student. When the war ended, Miriam was let go from her job. Her husband went back to dental school, and Miriam operated a small home-based business until he graduated.

For the next twenty years, Miriam raised their three children and did volunteer work in the community. She was the den mother for Cub Scouts, a Brownie leader, a room mother in the school, and a driver in too many carpools to mention—all activities that were expected of women in the postwar fifties.

When her youngest child entered kindergarten, Miriam realized she had to find a new direction. At the same time, she felt the social pressures to stay home, even though the children were all in school. None of her friends, now approaching forty, were inclined to go back to school or start a career. They thought it was a crazy idea, especially since Miriam's husband now had a flourishing dental practice and she could enjoy leisure and a comfortable lifestyle.

At thirty-nine, Miriam entered law school. She was one of three women in a class of 103, and she was twenty years older than the other students. The professors seemed to have a different standard for the women. She and the other women students were severely criticized for their mistakes, while the men were simply reminded of their errors. She worked harder to overcome their expressed doubts that she, an older woman, could make it. As a result of her hard work, she finished law school at the top of the class.

Another handicap was that as a woman—and an older woman—Miriam was out of "the system." The men had breakfast and lunch meetings and study groups. Important information was passed on in those groups. Notes were handed around to one another, past examinations were shared, cases were discussed. Miriam was not a part of it.

Meanwhile, Miriam's old friends grew weary of asking her to join them for lunch, dinner, the theatre, the club. They were miffed that she never had time to entertain any more, and they stopped asking her to their parties. Her parents felt neglected, too, and they let her know that she was doing something women didn't do—especially women of her social position.

Being left out of the male network continued to be a problem after graduation. Despite her academic achievements and honors, she was not offered a job. She opened her own office, only to discover that law school had not prepared her for the work world. In those days, lawyers depended on shared information from experienced lawyers for their practical advice. Miriam, standing alone, learned "on the job."

After eleven years in practice, Miriam ran for the position of judge. Still an outsider, again she was the target of criticism from male lawyers—but she won! She has served as a judge since the early 1970s.

Miriam says, "The most important ingredient for success in a career is a strong goal. If you know what you want and are firm about it, you can achieve it in spite of tremendous obstacles. It also helps to have a negative goal—to know what you *don't* want, the kind of life you see other women leading. If your goal is not strong, you can easily be deflected by your first rejection."

WOMEN *CAN* SUCCEED!

With enough motivation, women can have successful careers—but they have to work for their success, often harder than men. Do they pay a high personal price? You bet they do! At every turn they have to make hard choices, and sometimes they lose valued friends and husbands. Some may have to modify their professional goals in order to keep their marriages afloat, or for the children. Combining career and family obligations requires a great deal of juggling and setting of priorities. Sometimes it leaves no time at all to relax, to read for pleasure, or even to get enough sleep! But for many women, the cost of *not* trying is far higher. The woman over fifty can plunge ahead, being aware of the extra obstacles she faces, but knowing also that she has an extra depth to give to her work. The effort can result in stimulating and satisfying work that enriches her life.

CHAPTER EIGHT ⟩❦

Special Relationships

THE MEN IN OUR LIVES

How magnificent, how strong, how exciting was Prince Charming for the young woman who now is middle-aged. No personal sacrifice was too great for such a man. Parents, friends, relatives, career, all took a big step into the background. Loving him, making a home for him, helping him in his career became her priorities.

Popova, the widow in Chekhov's play, *The Bear*, described her love for her bridegroom. "I loved him passionately with all my being, as only a young intellectual woman can love. I gave him my youth, my happiness, my life, my fortune; he was my life's breath. I worshipped him as if I were a heathen."

After her husband's death, she discovered a desk full of love letters from women. The widow Popova continues her musings. "What good did it do? This best of men himself deceived me shamelessly at every step of the way."

Sarah Lerner, herself a widow and an observer of life, believes that a similar disillusionment about husbands is the real root of many women's crises at middle age. Sarah's observation fits Carl Jung's comments about men's new needs at midlife: The business world satisfied him all this while, but now he sees it as cutthroat and inconsiderate of human needs. Many men reach an intolerable level of frustration, and at forty, fifty, even sixty, the anger spills out. Men become prone to temper fits. Sometimes they have trouble with the boss, to the point of losing their jobs; or they turn to love affairs or alcohol. The older wife realizes he is not Prince Charming after all. As painful as this recognition is, it can be strengthening—*if* she realizes she must do something on her own to become individuated from her husband. Living through another person turns out not to work. When midlife crisis turns into divorce or widowhood, the love relationship with a man is over.

A *Cruise Isn't* The Love Boat

"Why do you think we take cruises? Why do we take classes, raid the cosmetic counters? Who do you think this is for—other women?"

Linda Mobley leaned toward me, an urgent plea in her voice, to tell me how it really is. We were in the lounge of a cruise ship. Linda is in her mid-seventies, traveling alone. There is a brittleness about her; anger welled up as she reflected on her single life. She talked about the multi-million-dollar beauty business, the $90 wrinkle creams that promise wonders, the luxurious spas, the expensive coiffures from exclusive salons. The beauty business reflects the eagerness that translates into desperation to attract male attention.

Some women of that age may be more relaxed about their lack of male companionship, but not all women—certainly not Linda. The odds slip dramatically as women outlive men in their seventies, three to one.

Many older widows don't want to get married again. They fear that remarriage will mean looking after a man sooner or later—a role they have had quite enough of. But they don't remember signing up to join a nunnery, either!

Linda found a group of compatible women on the ship. "It's good to talk to people of similar interests if you have no man around. If you have male companionship, you forget all that. If he wants to go here or there, you go." Not every woman would agree that she would drop her personal autonomy to hang onto a man—but others would, and not be so frank about saying it.

Linda has been a widow for twenty-six years. "I feel dead sexually," she laments. She is "on hold" but will come to life if a man comes her way. She feels defeated after years of trying for male attention. "I want to feel a part of the world, but I'm relegated to this." True, she is on a luxury cruise ship, not in a back alley searching for bread; but emotionally she is sacked.

Linda asks, "Instead of counseling women who have no male attention, why can't society provide some?" Couple situations tend to be "tight" and unresponsive to friendly overtures. Other women echoed the observation that a single woman—any single woman—causes a married woman to freeze and exit, taking her husband with her. "You don't show your rare diamonds to a diamond collector," says Linda wryly. "He might never let you alone as he inveigles to get the diamonds." As for single men—they seem to get swooped up immediately and taken off somewhere, out of harm's way. An unattached man wouldn't dare come on a cruise like this, is the opinion of the single women on board.

Sarah Lerner, the happier and more fulfilled woman on the same cruise, decries the attitudes that Linda expresses. "A widow needs to develop as an independent person. She needs to follow her interests and set new goals. It's a mistake to spend precious time looking for another hitching post," declares Sarah.

It is regrettable for the older woman that men are such a scarce commodity. The competition is keen, and women feel they must wage a full-scale campaign to have any male companionship at all. Perhaps cruise ships, churches, social groups of all kinds, could do more to make this possible. Folk dances, many of them circle dances, enable women without partners to join the dancing. In England there are pubs with long wooden tables to encourage people to socialize. Restaurants could have similar special tables for singles. As Linda pointed out, these women do have money, and they represent a new market—a large market, at that, since 40 percent of women over age sixty are alone.

On the cruise, the purser assigned the seating in the dining room. Linda was placed at a table with a romantic eighteen-year-old couple. They froze. Linda felt in the way, and the young couple silently agreed. She spoke to the purser about a new table. This time she got a young married couple with three children. The wife said, "I'm so glad you're at our table. You can help me keep the children in line." Linda made haste to change tables again. The next table had six couples. Linda turned to the man at her left and requested the salt. "The wife looked daggers at me!" Linda told the purser she had given up and wished to take meals alone in her stateroom. The purser asked for suggestions. "Could you seat the single people together at a table?" she asked. He did, putting together a table with men and women of different ages who were traveling alone. Linda had a great trip after all!

Marriage and the Older Woman

If masculine attention is so important to women, does that mean a married woman is in the best situation?

Yes, and no. When marriage works, it works very well. Usually it is an important support system for the late middle-aged and elderly person. Not that marriages are free of problems, but do they provide benefits—help, encouragement, someone to share concerns, someone to tell about the traffic jam on the way home. A wife who is in a reasonably good marriage has emotional support and a certain measure of financial security. She has a sexual partner—no small advantage, considering that after menopause women often increase their enjoyment of sex. Some husbands, with dimming vision and memories of their youth, tell their wives they are beautiful, and age doesn't seem to exist—at least some of the time.

The mutual caring system that is a natural part of marriage is another advantage. Social workers who deal with older couples are inspired by the dedication that husbands and wives have for each other. "Grow old along with me, the best is yet to be," is cross-stitched, framed, and hanging on the wall of many homes they visit. For those who have been able to achieve a compatible marriage, the adage can become a reality. A husband and wife can form a closeness that was not possible when they were so involved with children and careers. With retirement comes a social equality. After all these years, they are the same—two people trying to live as fully as possible. Moreover, they now have a common crisis to deal with—aging. This crisis can make personal issues fade into the background. They have a common enemy, society, to the extent that it impinges on their particular circumstance. The Medicare system, employers, relatives, professionals, the man at the delicatessen counter who served the young woman first even though they were next in line, the driver who wouldn't help them into the van—whoever is not responsive to their ever-increasing needs is the enemy. There is a second, related, mutual enemy—aging itself. The man's prostate surgery, the woman's diabetes, all the pain and aggravation and worry of it, can be shared. There is nothing that cements a relationship as quickly as a common adversary. The aging husband and wife give each other the encouragement they need to face the aggravation one more day.

When It's Bad, It's Horrid   Beware, however, of the marriage that has become embittered and troubled. Late middle age in such a marriage can be difficult, and old age can be unendurable. Retirement, after all, brings couples closer together, often for long hours at a time. This calamity happens at a time in life when, in many cases, there are fewer opportunities for other activities. Later, when illness, reduced finances, and no transportation occur, it can be a living hell. What can be worse than two people trapped in a small apartment, blaming each other for their predicament, their failings? At one time, people at sixty figured there wasn't much time left, so why not stick it out? But not with twenty or thirty more years ahead! Social Security does enable older people to live alone. It may be important for you to make your break now, whenever "now" occurs in your life.

A long-term marriage gives people many years to avoid finding out who they are. Unresolved conflicts about parents and early-life trauma get played out in the scene of the marriage. Along with this can come a kind of enmeshment, a feeling that stifles individual growth. Growth is possible in marriage, more so than in a life dedicated only to oneself. Nevertheless, it also is possible to avoid growth in marriage by subscribing everything to your spouse.

Sometimes there seems to be an unevenness about the

growth that does occur. A young wife and mother who has her hands full finds that she must postpone personal goals in order to care for her family. Children often leave mothers without the time or energy to do much else than care for them. If a young mother also has an outside job, she is close to burnout all the time. Motherhood itself is a growth experience. It teaches empathy, responsibility, enabling, and giving. But it doesn't serve to develop other parts of a mother's personality. Women who now are in late middle age also made tremendous personal sacrifices for their husbands so their careers could get off the ground. This was for a solid economic reason, not just a sexist one. Women could be hired in the 1950s, but at a minimal salary, while men were able to find jobs at salaries that supported a family on their income alone. So the young wife answered her husband's telephone, made dinner, cared for the home and children, and generally made it possible for him to concentrate on work. That kind of sacrifice put difficult emotional burdens on both husband and children. The husband may appreciate it for years. How else could he have developed a successful medical practice or taken an executive position that involved travel? How could he have been elected to political office, without an unpaid loyal supporter to help him and run the household as well?

Men get themselves in a box, too. From childhood they are programmed to have their entire lives tied up in their jobs. The heavy responsibility of marriage and family reinforces the old conditioning. Wives contribute to the pressure in that their standard of living is totally dependent on the husband's earning capacity—or was thought to be, a few decades ago. Wives take care of the couple's social life, the children's problems, anything resembling emotional work. Sometimes wives take over the entire emotional experience, or their husbands hand it to them. We find men who are unable to express feelings, married to women who are deluged with feeling, their own *plus* his on an unconscious level. Suddenly in late midlife, men realize the pressures of family, marriage, and employers have taken them in directions they didn't want to go. "What happened to the part of me that always wanted to climb a mountain? To write a novel?" They lose their tight sense of identity. A wife already may have started her struggle to redefine herself and find a new role. Thus it is not surprising to find mutual resentments. Both have been pressed for years to go down paths that have not led to the life satisfaction they expected. Instead, both men and women say at this point, "Is this all there is?" Blaming each other is a natural step. How could they not? In a way, they were both the products of circumstance, of each other. Each has been using the marriage to avoid the important personal issues. They had expected to keep them squelched forever; but at middle age the hormones are shifting, life is shifting, and the issues rise to the surface. Therapists call this process in a marriage "collusion." It need not be a permanent affliction. There are two ways to break collusion: divorce, or therapy that promotes the internal independence of each person. It is painful either way.

Many factors come into play in determining whether or not a marriage is salvageable. How deep is the collusion? How willing to change are the partners? What positive elements exist in the marriage?

Some marriages should be refurbished, some ended. How do you tell the difference? This is very difficult. Any close marriage has conflict, a kind of love/hate, dependence/independence struggle. Couples who have not argued much have a dead marriage on their hands—maybe innocuous, but deadly dreary. Extreme cases of misery are easy to spot, but middling amounts of misery are hard to evaluate.

A New Stress on Marriage   There is a new stress on marriage today, notes therapist Gypsy Lyle. People's tolerance of discord has been altered. "For better or worse," we used to say. Nowadays, with divorce common and acceptable, there is a limit to how much worse we want to go with. Still, life is full of many stresses and difficulties. To run off at the onset of trouble is not to be truly married at all.

Sometimes it is hard to judge when you are merely "going through a phase" in your marriage. Unless your marriage is obviously either blissful or tortured, this is an important time in your life to assess it with a marriage counselor. Some researchers believe that more than half of retired couples have miserable marriages, which affects the health as well as the happiness of both the man and the woman. Often a seemingly miserable marriage can be put on course and turned into a satisfying one.

Can you afford to have marriage counseling? You can't afford not to! Look for public agencies with counseling services, or choose health insurance policies that have good mental health coverage. They cost more, but not as much as the ill health that a miserable life will cause you. Use savings or borrow money, but take care of yourself in this way to ensure your future happiness.

"My husband would never go for counseling." Many men avoid physicians, therapists, anything that smacks of asking someone else for help. These are the men who drive in circles rather than ask for directions. But have you asked your husband lately? He may have begun to suffer his own identity crisis. A classmate dies, and he realizes he doesn't have forever to find a good life. Now, when he comes home, he wants to find a refuge as never before. Perhaps this feeling is more in tune with your distress than you know. He, too, is beginning to realize that retirement and aging will increase his need for a happy home. He sees his wife becoming more assertive with age, and there are frequent skirmishes over decisions as she tries to change the balance of power in her favor. Just as he wants peace and contentment the most, it seems out of grasp. He may go for help willingly. In any case, this may well be the time to tell him, "No more Mrs. Nice Guy! I need some counseling, and I expect you to go, too, to see what can be done to make our lives better."

The stakes are high. Marriage is a plus for the older person, and it should not be given up lightly. Deciding about this may be the biggest gamble of your life. A woman who is divorced at sixty or more may feel devastated by loneliness, low income, and the loss of a mate. It is far easier for a man to find female companionship. On the other hand, women who need to make the break, and do it, find a new lease on life, new freedom, and a chance for happiness. It's all in knowing yourself.

Retirement and Marriage

Take a high-powered business executive who is accustomed to making quick decisions and issuing orders to his staff; then give him a gold watch and send him home. His wife, Queen of the Home, awaits. What transpires shouldn't be so unpredictable. It's like sending a bull into a china shop.

In his book, *The Reality of Retirement*, Jules Z. Willing writes about what happens when a successful businessman retires to a household with a wife who is equally successful in her field, homemaking. Men start to believe that their goals at work were the same as personal goals. Power breakfasts, meetings, mergers, all took up his total time and energy. The family's role was to adjust to second billing and assist him by having things run smoothly at home. "Don't bother your father. He has a report to write." This was often necessary for their own well-being, dependent as they were on his salary. "If he sinks, we is sunk." When the husband is asked for his advice on a serious problem, he does what he does at work—he calls for expedient and conclusive action, calling this "decision making." He fails to realize that the problems at home are not like the problems at work; they are human problems of people whose needs are just as important as those of the executive husband and father. They require empathy and caring, a focusing not on the problem but on the people who have the problem. There is no "bottom line," no "unit cost factor"—just the human condition.

A wife may adjust to this situation during the busy working years, but she balks at this corporate behavior during retirement. This "take charge" kind of person tackles his retirement like a project, and he sees his unwitting wife as the staff assigned to help him complete it. He assumes she will answer the phone, sort the mail, and write any letters he may want to send. The wife, meanwhile, has been exploring her own individuality, and she insists on her share of the power in the family. She has her own activities, the bridge club meets at her home, and she's making a quilt. She hadn't counted on making him lunch, much less helping him organize his time and do projects. The scene is set for explosion.

Yet, it *is* possible for a couple to make the needed changes. Obviously, many do or there would be even more divorces at this point.

Sometimes it takes quite a bit of creativity to work out a workable solution. Take the case of Janet and Jim Wells. Janet couldn't say, "Hey, you're bugging me," and the first three years after Jim's retirement were almost impossible. Jim had been a psychologist. He was weary of listening to other people's problems, and now he wanted someone to listen to him. That someone was Janet. "Look," he told her, "I've worked all these years and I've been away from you a lot. I haven't shared with you as much as I should. Now I want to share." He began telling her about the frustrations he had experienced as a psychologist and now was experiencing in retirement. He became absorbed in his health problems, and he gave her a running account. He didn't realize that his sharing put such a burden on Janet, who was establishing herself as a community organizer. "I'm not retired," she said. Like many professional men, Jim was uneasy about joining groups of people he did not consider his "peers." Janet finally realized she had to spend more time away from him. His sharing was burdening her, and she realized that his depression was "catching." Jim and Janet worked out a unique system that allows both to retain their individuality. Janet lives in an apartment about an hour's drive from Jim. He visits her on weekends, and they have a lovely romantic relationship, all the more satisfying because of her increased autonomy.

Retirement can interfere with what a woman wants to do about her own life. She may be trying to cope with her own personal identity crisis. Men often want to move to the lake country where they can fish, or sell the house and buy an RV. It isn't possible for the woman to get a Ph.D., hold down a job, or do volunteer work, while rolling across the country in an RV. It also is difficult to maintain her personal support system, the group of friends she has built up over the years. Friendship, support groups, all are important in facing the difficulties that life brings. Although the wife has been her husband's chief support over the years, usually it hasn't been a two-way street. Most wives look to other women for the emotional empathy they require. Unless seeing the country has been her priority also, the RV solution works against her.

When the Single Woman Retires   In some respects, the single woman is more fortunate. She can pursue her life in whatever way she prefers. Single women also have the advantage of experience in being their own person, without all the emotional pressures of husband and children and without the dependency issues. These same years of personal freedom have enabled her to follow her career path without guilt, interruptions, and complications.

But single women have fears of loneliness and dependency as they age. Years of competency in the business or professional world have not prepared them for the drastic changes that retirement brings. They suddenly realize that most of their friends were work-related. When the job ends, most of the friendships fade away. Not having a family and not building friendships around other interests leaves these women open and vulnerable to loneliness.

Women who have maintained their careers, whether single or married, usually want to retire earlier, at about sixty-two. They may find the business world increasingly tense, and they start thinking about leisure opportunities they have missed. Conversely, the woman whose children have left the nest and who finds a new career in the business world usually is too enthusiastic about her work to want to retire. At sixtysomething, it becomes very difficult to give up the job that has brought her a new lease on life.

Eileen Feuerbach, who studied women and retirement, found that two-thirds of them enjoyed retirement, but one-third were unhappy. "That is a lot of women to be unhappy," comments Eileen.

Further Thoughts on Men

It really does seem to be a man's world. That is the consensus among late-middle-aged women. This cultural trend is reflected in the women's frustrating careers, reduced economic circumstances, and other kinds of disappointments.

Don't think of men as being villains. They are programmed to have their entire lives tied up in their work.
The wife traditionally has taken care of the couple's social
life and brought cultural and creative interests to the home.
Men are unprepared for a change in status as they age.
Annette watched her husband suffer the letdown of a business change. She watched his blood pressure get higher and
higher as his frustrations mounted. Then another firm took
over his company. While he was frantically worrying about
what he would do with his life, he died.

Doris Reed notes, "Men have a hard life. They have
taken upon themselves the business of running the world.
They need the help of women. They have defeated themselves by not accepting that help." Men are beginning to
accept women's contributions as being equal to their own,
but it is a slow process of acceptance.

OUR ADULT CHILDREN

Adult children can be an unexpected bonus in life.
This generation of late-middle-agers usually didn't experience the freewheeling exchange of ideas between generations, the easy companionship that can exist between parent
and child. Turn-of-the-century parents kept their children
at a respectful arm's length. They had expectations, and
their children fulfilled them. No one asked if the children
had feelings or wishes. Many women I talked with remarked, "Our parents lost us." They knew their role as disci-
plinarians, but they had no idea of how to get along with an
adult child as an equal. It is to the credit of men and women
of this generation that they are able to shift gears. They do
talk freely with their children, and as a reward they get to
know the former children as people and caring friends.

Does the Relationship Need Improvement?

Women of this generation who don't hear much from their children express sorrow and disappointment. Sometimes women who have concentrated exclusively on their families feel that something is owed them. Just what is owed them, if anything, is difficult to determine. Most people do believe that adult children owe their parents respect and at least some appreciation. This implies some sort of contact (although not necessarily frequent) by telephone, letter, or personal visit.

For many young adults, the relationship is painful, especially as they find their own place in the world and perhaps discover that the parental messages they received at home turned out to be inadequate. What should they do?

More pertinent here is the question, "What can a parent do to improve the situation?"

Motherhood is a role of contradiction. Children are to be nurtured, given values, held close. Through tantrums, illness, nightmares, failures, rebellions, a mother holds fast to her dream of what her child can be. At the same time, successful mothering demands a letting go, an absence of manipulation to let the son or daughter become what the mother hoped he or she would be.

One father said, "Just when they get fit to live with, they live with someone else." The parents see the child through the careless immaturity of the child, but they don't always reap the full benefit of the mature adult. The parent may still think of the thirty- or forty-year-old son as the same person who dented the fender on the family car at age sixteen. If so, adult communication will be difficult.

There is still another complication. This is an age of extreme individualism. Books are written about how to take care of yourself; therapists are consulted if the behavior of other people causes discomfort. Many people believe that the present younger generations are self-involved and uncaring about the needs of others. Today's late-middle-aged generation may have unwittingly created this situation, by focusing intensely on their children's needs to the neglect of their own. The postwar generations of children were raised in the suburbs. But suburban life creates an artificial, age-segregated environment. It is not "the real world." Those young adults may still lack connections with older people, people of other economic levels and other races. Their view of the world may be fragmented, broken only by sentimentalized television specials about the neglected groups in this society.

Be that as it may, the important issue is what to do now. Should we sit at home and wait for the telephone to ring? No, not that. Should we berate the son or daughter for never calling? Should we call and tell them we are sick when the true situation is minor?

If you are feeling neglected by your children, what you want is to feel appreciated for yourself alone. A prod meant to increase guilt is doomed to failure. How do you feel about people who make you feel guilty and inferior? Not like ringing them on the phone!—more like wringing their necks! Chances are, those adult children already do feel guilty. It is difficult to forget that you have a mother. Even the most egocentric business tycoon must think about it, at times.

There are several possibilities for improving the situation. Let's look at them.

Come to Terms with Your Situation   Women do sacrifice themselves for their children. Sadly, the children seldom realize this until they are parents themselves—and nowadays, this situation is slow in coming. Young children would be more fun if their toys weren't always scattered about, their bibs always caked with oatmeal, their diapers always dirty.

While this is true, it also is basically true that women choose to be mothers of their own free will. What work can be more important to an individual and to society? What is more creative than the birth of a new life? It is an honored vocation.

Confusion enters the picture here, as many women admit they did not experience this decision (at least in retrospect) as "free will." It's true that society expected this kind of dedication to the family. Our role model on our early TV screens was Mother, the devoted homemaker in "Father Knows Best." It also is true that methods of birth control were less dependable, and there was great debate about its morality. Women chose not to defy society; and that was their "free will" decision—to conform. The pressures to live that life came from many sources; but women need to remember that the pressures were not from the children themselves. The children just *arrived*, unaware of the social expectations of the day. They absorbed their parents' values. The parents sent them to college "to make something of themselves." They did. It was what we wanted them to do. "You want more?" asks Rachel Zane. "Get it from your peers."

Women do need something from their children, although perhaps it is not what they tend to expect. Accepting that your life of self-denial is not the children's fault is a first step toward achieving a closer relationship with them. Remembering that it was not complete self-denial also helps. Watching children grow is one of life's greatest pleasures. By releasing the children from blame, you can ease up on the pressure of expectations.

Develop Your Own Personality   Exploring new horizons for yourself also frees you from needing so much appreciation from your children. Already you have accomplished life's greatest task. Does the climber of Mt. Everest also have to become a movie star to be appreciated? But current society

values people for what they are accomplishing *today*. Iron-
ically, improving your own life may enhance your relationship with the children. As a woman increases her interests,
the children become more interested in her. It is not pleasant to visit a mother whose main interest in life seems to be
how you are raising her grandchildren.

Initially, adult children may see their branching-out
mother as "selfish"—but not for long. When a mother is
ever-sacrificing, never having fun, it makes growing up look
very tiresome. A parent who has strong interests is far more
interesting. Mother becomes more concerned about when
the next bird-watching trip takes place than when her son
last called—and the son becomes more interested in calling!

Learn New Communication Skills   In the beginning, parents are
larger, stronger, more intelligent than their children. It is
the parents' duty to tell their children about the world. This
parental duty creates an imbalance of power. As children
grow and learn on their own, they want to establish their
own feelings of power. But some parents wish to hold onto
their power base. Suggestions become commands, criticism
becomes condemnation. Even observations about political
candidates can be given as if the parents think they still
know best. Unless parents recognize this, they will never
have the closeness to their children that they desire.

Women are learning "power talk" in order to adapt to
the business and professional world. Adult children, ultra-
sensitive to a loaded power deck, may require Mother to
step back into *anti*power talk. A little less certainty in the
tone of voice, more frequent qualifying phrases, may give
adult children the feeling that their opinions count, too.

1. Be careful with compliments. Make sure there is no
   "but"—no curve ball that follows. "You look nice in that
   dress, but you really should lose weight." Looking

nice in that dress also may sound like a value judgment, implying she doesn't look so good in her other clothes.

2. If suggestions are made (very risky at best!), make sure they are tentative and combined with a lot of active listening. Avoid the word *should*. Not, "You should move to a safer neighborhood"; instead, "I worry that your neighborhood isn't safe. Do you think it is?"

3. Completely avoid criticism! The new wife may be a disappointment, the new apartment a dump, the new hairdo unbecoming, but eventually the adult child will realize it without Mother pointing it out. Also, you could be wrong! There are extreme situations, like child abuse and wife beating, that call for strong measures; but ordinary situations do not.

4. Avoid trivializing your adult children's concerns. Their choice of an occupation, or anything else, is just that— their choice. It is not for you to decide what is important to any individual. "Junior might flunk fifth grade" may not sound urgent to you as you await the results of your breast biopsy, but Junior's situation is foremost and upsetting to Junior's parents.

5. Avoid direct questions. Most people resent them. Suppose a friend stops by and grills you with questions. "Where were you last Sunday when I called? When are you coming to see me? Why did you let your son drive his tricycle in the alley?" You would feel that your privacy is being invaded. Your children feel this way, but doubly so because you are the parent.

6. Once in a while, say, "But I could be wrong." It sounds as if there's not much you *can* say. Not so. When your closest friend comes by, you find a lot to talk about— the news, your activities, his or her activities. It is a pleasant relationship because you are not busy judging each other. The friend may have faults, but that doesn't spoil the pleasure of the conversation.

Your adult children feel your power plays acutely, even when you are unaware of what you are doing. Become aware. Pretend that the adult child is your closest friend. Perhaps then, the child will feel safe enough to become one.

7. Don't be a judge. Communication flows freely between friends when they are not judging each other. It is hard to overcome this tendency when it was your job for so many years to evaluate your child's behavior. "Isn't it time he was toilet trained? Is she spending enough time on homework? Will playing football injure him? Is she learning good social skills?"

The children are grown up now. It is simply too late for judgments and evaluations. He may have a lot to learn, as do we all; but now he has other ways of learning. He has professors, employers, mentors, and the hard road of experience to teach him. Unless he's going skydiving without a parachute, it's best to let him decide about it.

A judgment becomes an attack. An attack leads to counterattack by the child—and off you go into a full-scale battle. Or you have a child who prefers not to telephone.

Cindy Ellis, a thirty-six-year-old journalist, has developed a technique for defusing her parents' judgments so that she doesn't feel wounded and angry. When her mother expresses a judgment, Cindy imagines that her mother is a friend, perhaps an older friend, who is saying the same thing.

"Jimmy needs new shoes," when coming from her mother, sounds as if Cindy is neglecting her child and has no sense of responsibility. "Jimmy needs new shoes," when coming from the friend, is more along the lines of simple fact. It may be a bit of an intrusion, but it is not worthy of a full-scale depression or attack. Cindy probably would look at the shoes and say, "Yes, I plan to get some as soon as I have time to shop." It wouldn't take her five days to recover.

This technique can be done in reverse. If your daughter wears her hair upright in a streak of green, smile and pretend that she is the daughter of a friend. If your son has "dropped out of the system" and is making wood sculptures in the Baja, pretend that he, too, is a friend. Wouldn't it be fun to know someone who makes wood sculptures in the Baja? Of course! What a marvelous tour of the Baja you could have with such a connection! You could be friends with any woodcarver in the Baja if he weren't your son! And that is the point. Why not enjoy a deep friendship with your son?

Children, too, are judgmental, and sometimes they are quick to criticize what *you* do. Would you mind the criticism from someone else? "Why don't you learn to balance the checkbook, Mom?" If your accountant or therapist asked the question, it might be merely a fact of life. You have known for years that life would be smoother if you could manage to figure out the finances.

Does antipower talk sound phony? No more so than the assertive talk of the business world. Both are facets of the personality. If a parent has a strong need for power over the child, any techniques will be useless. There is a premise here: that the power plays are mostly habit, a carryover from when the parent had to save a two-year-old from the perils of the street. For a parent who seeks out power deliberately, these techniques will not sound convincing anyway.

Make It Safe to Tell All   When adult children are not communicating with their parents at all, chances are they are burdened with a lot of resentment about the past. They also may be burdened with guilt. They know very well that the parents remember a former foolish behavior that hardly ever gets discussed openly. There is a reason. Often it is not really *safe* to unburden yourself with a parent. Revealing too many feelings could bring on more of the dreaded criticism and judgment.

Perhaps after many months of improved communication skills and developing the habit of not judging, enough tension may dissolve so that the parent and adult child can explore the issue. A family therapist may be needed. Misconceptions and misunderstandings arise easily. They need to be resolved. Late middle age is the time to do it, in case you're not up to it at eighty. Children may say nothing about their hurts in an effort to protect the parent. Consider whether you want this protection now, or if you would like to know what is wrong and can handle the knowledge without increasing your anger toward the child.

Make sure it really is safe—that you can accept the criticism and feel strong enough to hear it without resorting to angry counterattack that will further injure the relationship. Make sure also that the child is not just "dumping" frustrations on you, but is sincerely and sensitively trying to mend the relationship.

Cindy Ellis says, "I think my parents have not forgiven me for the anguish I put them through in the sixties when I was living on the streets, high on drugs." Cindy doesn't know how to bridge the distance between them. Situations in her early childhood led her to experiment with drugs. She would like to talk about those situations, but she is afraid that if she mentions the incidents, her parents might take it as more criticism and block off all communication.

Several women in the over-fifty generation also confided that the turmoil they experienced with their teenage children in the sixties was so severe that it has not been forgotten. "He was always one step from the law," one mother recalls. "I don't know if I have forgiven him. I wish we could talk about it."

And these are the children of the parents who had tried harder than any previous generation of parents to meet the needs of their offspring!

Respect One Another   The mother-child bond is a strong one, and it can be an impetus for both to understand and respect each other. Respect for one's independence, autonomy, values, privacy, and chosen lifestyle obviously needs to go both ways. Society has changed so dramatically that today it can be very difficult for parents and adult children to understand one another. How is the mother, who was a virgin on her wedding day, to fully understand her sexually emancipated daughter?

Consider that children today are the product of their society, just as we were when young. Although today they have so much more exposure to the ways of the world, they still are *young*. They may not be self-aware and self-sufficient enough to be able to make life decisions based on their inner needs, any more than we were. They are influenced by their friends and the current cultural trends in making decisions about their lives. Yet youth is the *time* for these decisions to be made. We must realize that underneath their puzzling behavior are the same struggles and uncertainties that we experienced, and many of the same basic values.

The Returnees

More and more young adults are returning home after an unsuccessful encounter with the outside world. This can cause turmoil when it interrupts the fifty- or sixty-year-old mother's newfound freedom. The lack of privacy impedes her, and she asks testily, "When is it my turn?"

Other women enjoy this protracted motherhood. These women usually have large houses, and they are assertive enough to work out equitable arrangements so their needs are met, too. The returnees need to understand that the ground rules have changed from when they were little children. Now they must respect their parents' new need for autonomy.

Expectations for the Future

When healthy mothers who have not planned for this next stage of life expect their children somehow to fill in the gap, that is another matter. One such mother, a widow, moved to another city to be near her daughter. Once there, she neglected to seek out friends of her own. She calls her daughter constantly about her needs. The resentful daughter is already overburdened with her own family, but she doesn't know how to approach her mother to talk about the problem.

Young adults who are busy establishing themselves in career and child raising have an identity crisis, too. It is difficult to feel responsible for an adult parent, especially when that parent is healthy enough to be independent and is not really all that old. The situation doesn't lead to the close, friendly relationships that bring so much pleasure into older adults' lives. Neither is it constructive for the young adult to expect the late-middle-aged parents to continue to meet the son's or daughter's needs. It is fine if the older parents can afford to give children money to help, but this should be done with caution. The older parents don't have that many years to replenish their financial reserves. A kind of truce needs to be called during these years, while both generations solve their concurrent identity problems and learn to relate to each other as fellow adults.

What to expect in old age is still another issue. So much

depends on the situation of both the parents and the adult children. A lot depends, too, on what governmental decisions are made about catastrophic health care and Social Security provisions, and about the development of home care resources and more caring kinds of nursing homes. Most women want to remain independent physically, financially, and emotionally as long as possible. Still, they like the security of knowing that an adult child would be there for them, for whatever unknown need they might have. Many women hope they will never require constant physical care from a child. They have wretched memories of their own parents' dependency, and they don't want their own children to have that kind of memory of them.

What Adult Daughters Wish They Could Tell Their Mothers

A professional woman in her late thirties wishes her conversations with her mother weren't so demoralizing. She shares with us what she wishes she could tell her mother, but doesn't dare.

1. Don't be jealous of me. Most careers are not as glamorous as they look on television. Many of us hate our jobs. Life as a career woman and a mother is extremely hectic. Many of us wish we had the luxury of staying home and being totally supported by a husband, as you did. But today it takes two incomes to have a family.
2. Appreciate my work. You seem interested in how I raise my son, but not in what my office work is like.
3. Remember that there is more than one way to raise a child. You be your kind of parent and let me be my kind of mother. If I do something different, it's not meant as an insult to you.

4. Hey, I am still your child! I'm glad you love your grandchildren, but I could use your love, too. Why do
   you say, "Only the children matter now"? It's not all
   over. Don't you matter? Don't I matter? It's hard to
   compete with a cute, curly-haired three-year-old.
5. Let me feel safe enough to talk with you about the
   things in our relationship that are wrong. We both seem
   to avoid being open with one another. I would really
   like to be close. I know you would, too. But my past
   experiences with you have shown me that it just isn't
   safe. You seem to feel I should be a problem already
   solved—not a changing, evolving person in a relationship that needs work.

What Middle-Aged Mothers Would Like Their Adult Children to Know

The older mothers also wish closeness with their
daughters and hesitate to speak about it in person.

1. Wherever you are, I have been there. I remember the
   uncertainties of being twenty, the overburdened stress
   of being thirty, the "Is this all there is?" fears of being
   forty. Now at fifty, sixty, seventy, I have new concerns.
   Now I have the "Is this all there is?" feeling *in spades*. But
   still, I do remember. And even though you have chosen
   a path that is vastly different from mine, I can understand more about what you are going through than you
   think.
2. Don't envy my current freedom or lifestyle. I had the
   same pressures, responsibilities, and restrictions that you
   now have. Eating bonbons in front of the TV all day is
   one thing, but don't be misled by my apparent
   inactivity. The inward search is not so outwardly

visible as some lines of work, but it *is* work nevertheless. My Year or My Month requires time to read and dream, time to think. It is not "doing nothing."

3. I wish you would try to get to know me as a person, apart from my role as mother. We would have a lot more mutuality and a lot more fun together.

4. Life seems different at sixty. I am still the same person but somehow put together in a different way. It causes frustration for us both when you expect me to be the same person I was before. I get tired more easily and I don't handle stress as well as I used to, so I need to take better care of myself. If I spend more time on my personal care and pursuits, it doesn't mean I don't love you just as much as ever.

5. At fifty or sixty I am not yet disengaging from life—and at seventy or eighty I don't plan to, either. I may move more slowly, more tentatively, but that's arthritis, not disengagement. So don't write me off as history. I am still in the mainstream of life.

6. I guess I want it both ways, the being old and not-so-old. I hope you do realize that I will not live forever. You and I need to get to know and appreciate each other while I'm still around.

7. I never thought I'd care about Mother's Day cards, but I find to my great surprise that I do. It's okay if it doesn't come on the exact date, but now and then send me a card—and add a personal message, please!

8. You say I botched up your life? If I did, it was with a loving concern for your welfare. Realize that I did the best I could. We all are raised by people who cannot predict the future and thus tend to repeat the past. My hope is that you will get on with your life, extract yourself from the negative (as I have had to do myself), and appreciate the positive things that I did for you.

OUR AGING PARENTS

Perhaps the most painful issue of all is that of aging parents. The new long life expectancy is so full of possibilities. A parent who is finally really "old" can be the fount of many kinds of wisdom—a retainer to the past and to the culture. Many middle-aged people enjoy their visits with parents who, while getting a bit forgetful or crotchety, are still vital people. An interesting, caring older person is a delight; but a difficult and angry one is quite something else.

We all hope that our bodies and minds will slink off around the same time in that inevitable final decline. But for many people, the timing is off and the mind becomes senile while the body remains strong. The medical system, which brought us this longevity, can perpetuate it seemingly forever. A senile lady of ninety-four who is unaware of her environment, aware only of her inner frustration and misery, is kept alive through pneumonia by antibiotics and modern technology's breathing equipment. The nursing home staff would not think of refusing care. But her children think of it, stressed out as they are by Mother's state of mind. It is painful to see someone you love be reduced to a kind of automaton, eating, sleeping, breathing, but having little connection with the world and probably wanting to die. Meanwhile, the nursing home costs may be impoverishing the family. Families need legal help in planning for catastrophic illness so that the estate can be preserved for the surviving husband or wife. This needs to be done *before* the nursing care is needed.

Even more difficult are the pre-nursing-home days. When a senile elder attempts to live with a fifty- or sixty-year-old son or daughter, the result can be disastrous. When an elderly parent is alert and is appreciative, living with an adult child sometimes works out. When the same parent is senile and critical, wandering about the neighborhood if not under constant guard, care becomes a burden. The adult son or daughter is not young either! As Eda LeShan points out in *Oh, To Be Fifty Again*, sixty or seventy is too old an age to bear the responsibility of taking care of another human being. Yet many try, thinking they have no choice.

The problem is increasing. A futurist said that today's young adults will spend more time caring for elderly relatives than for children. But child care is inherently more satisfying because the child is learning more each day and you can see the progress you and the child are making.

Still More Expectations of Women

Women have always been considered the caretakers. In earlier years, a grandparent often lived in a family home and experienced the care and concern of the middle-aged parents. It was the way people lived. Today, houses are smaller, servants are extremely rare, and the separate generations are accustomed to independence and privacy. Remembering the old days creates high expectations. The disappointment that occurs when the elderly parent realizes the reality of the situation leads to strong tensions. Today it is not a given presumption that the parents will move in; it is a matter to be carefully thought about, considering the needs of everyone in the family.

Sometimes it is the son who cares for his mother. Dan, a drama professor, wanted to care for his mother at home. She had give him much love and encouragement over the years, and he welcomed the chance to return something to her. Dan was not young himself, and the task became difficult. Yet at her death, Dan had the satisfaction of knowing that he was there with her until the end. Dan had not married and raised a family. Perhaps caretaking satisfied a long neglected need to give of himself for the benefit of someone else.

But usually the caretaker is the daughter, and the role comes at the worst possible time in her life. Her child-raising days are over, she and her husband are close to retirement, and they want to live the good life while they still can. Now look what's happened! And the person now restricting her is—guess who? The parent again! Fortunately, support groups for caretakers, men and women, are being formed all over the country. There is an awareness of the problems involved, and resources are being designed to give help. Contact the gerontology department of your medical center for more information.

Should Mother Live with Us?

Social worker Helen Briggs warns that a family should not take an elderly person into their home without some straight thinking and professional consultation. Not that it can't work out; but both parent and child should realize that the situation may change if the parent becomes senile and requires more care. One of the unmet needs of our society is guidance for adults who are dealing with aging parents.

When Joan Waring's mother became ill, Joan insisted that she come to live with her. There was an added incentive: Joan's husband had never done well financially, and they still lived in the same small bungalow they had moved into as newlyweds. They persuaded Joan's mother to sell her home and spend her savings to finance an attractive large home for all of them. Mother preferred to stay in her own home, but she gave in to her daughter's pleas. She had begun to worry about her increasing age and possible future infirmity, and she had always wanted to see Joan in a nicer house.

A few years later they noticed that Mother was clashing with Joan more and more in the kitchen, and she was just rocking away the rest of her time. She was beginning to be a burden and a care. Joan and her husband secretly made arrangements to enter her in a nursing home. They took her to the ocean on a vacation, and on the way back from the beach they drove to the nursing home, told her this was a good place to stay, and left her there. Mother not only had no say about her own destiny, but was placed in an inadequate, authoritarian kind of home. Deprived of all independence and autonomy, she declined rapidly. Joan laments, "When I go to see her, she won't speak to me."

This unhappiness could have been prevented. Their plans ended up meeting the needs of none of the people involved. They might have hired someone to help Mother so she could stay in her own home as she wanted to do. Or she could have considered moving closer to Joan's smaller home. As it turned out, she lost her independence and her power, which for an older person means being able to make choices and deciding about one's own life.

Many people panic at sixty or seventy. They need reassurance that they have a long and fulfilling life ahead of them. The adult children need to know that, too, so they can recognize the parents' potential and help them to find ways of staying independent for as long as possible.

Role Reversal

What hurts, of course, is that the parents who cared about us, who were there to help to the extent they could, are suddenly gone. In their stead are these frail, confused, older beings who seem not to be able to focus on our concerns, so great are their own. When I visited my mother in a nursing home, I asked the receptionist to tell her that her mother was here! It was a slip of the tongue, but rather accurate. The child becomes the parent, but the new "child"—the elderly one—is not accustomed to listening to the new "parent," and things can get quite difficult.

The older middle-agers are acutely aware that they are the next generation in line. To see the suffering of senility and the damage it does to the entire family is to fear it above all else. It is almost too much to talk about. Fortunately, it by no means happens to everyone. As reported by Ken Dychtwald in *Age Wave*, only 5 percent of people over the age of sixty-five are residing in nursing homes.

Communicating with Older Parents

Talking with a senile, difficult elderly parent can be the most trying situation the late-middle-aged child ever faces. Yesterday's parents didn't think about antipower talk or defusing the relationship or making an effort to establish an equalized one. They were authorities, and the children were to be subordinate. No matter that the child is now sixty or seventy. In fact, the power talk is apt to increase as the parent's fears and vulnerability intensify with age and illness.

It is up to the adult child to learn new ways of communication. *Getting Your Way—The Nice Way*, written by Carol C. Flax, Ph.D., and Earl Ubell, is a useful book. Flax and Ubell recommend that we learn to use nurturing listening skills combined with enough assertion to protect our own needs. This can be difficult, since many of the remarks made by aging parents are angry and defensive. It requires listening to what is said, stopping to pick up the underlying feeling (which often is one of hurt), and responding not with an attack but with a statement that acknowledges the parent's needs and also expresses the adult child's needs.

The middle-aged woman needs to separate herself emotionally from the parental barbs, even while she attempts to meet the parent's needs. This is done by:

1. *Reflective listening.* Really hearing what the parent is saying, repeating it to show you understand what was said.
2. *Responding with nurturing comments.* The parent is hurting, after all. Respond to that pain.
3. *Telling your side.* Expressing what you are able to do for them, and specifying the limits you need to set because of other priorities.

Resist a counterattack, which only intensifies the parent's anger. That doesn't mean you should give in to everything!

Here's what *not* to do:
Mother (*calling on the telephone*): Come over here right now.
You: Is something wrong?
Mother: Yes, something's wrong. My daughter doesn't care about me. After all the sacrifices I made for you!
You: Some sacrifice! You had a baby-sitter most of the time.
Mother: How dare you say that to me! You don't come to see me, you don't care. I just hope your daughter treats you that way some day. You'll be sorry.

Already, you *are* sorry. This conversation leaves you guilty and angry, and Mother unhappy. Try a new approach:

Mother: Come over here right now.
You: Is something wrong?
Mother: Yes, something's wrong. My daughter doesn't care about me.
You: You know I do care about you.

Mother: If you did, you would be over here. I bought one of those microwave meals for dinner, and I can't figure out the new microwave. I'm hungry.

You: That must be hard to be alone and hungry, with a new gadget to figure out.

Mother: So you'll come?

You: Look, I have to finish getting dinner on the table. Ed's boss is here and they are discussing an important business decision.

Mother: I'm not important? I looked after you when you had the mumps, but now I don't matter.

You: You *are* important. But so is Ed and the dinner. Make yourself a snack, and I'll be over in an hour to work on the microwave with you.

Mother: Well, okay. I'll see you later.

Dr. Susan Woods, a psychiatrist, at about age fifty finally stood up to her father. Father was an Old World authoritarian who commandeered the family. He was the captain; they were the crew. Susan had always been intimidated by him. Even her psychiatric training didn't enable her to confront her father's demands.

One day she got a call from her father. "Come here at once, Susan. I am sick."

Susan was on her way to the hospital for an emergency. She was familiar with her father's medical condition, and the new symptoms didn't sound like a serious problem. So she said, "I can't come right now, Dad."

"You come over here! Now!"

"Dad, I've got an emergency here. Why do I have to come over there instantly?"

"Because you are my daughter."

Susan saw her opening. "Dad, I am your daughter. But I am also a doctor, a wife, and a mother. I have to give priority to what seems the most urgent, and right now it's my patient who needs me. I'll be over as soon as I can see my way clear."

Father stopped his domination, and Susan asserted her individuality and independence. Everyone's needs were met.

It does help to be a doctor en route to an emergency; everyone appreciates that. But every woman has priorities of her own, too. While those priorities may not sound vital to the outside world, they are important to her and they should be honored.

Relationships are vital to a woman's happiness. It is a challenge to nourish them and at the same time seek one's own destiny.

CHAPTER NINE

Relating to Our Doctors

MEDICAL CARE

To ask a middle-aged woman about her medical care sometimes unleashes an avalanche of grievances. She is old enough to remember the old-fashioned doctor who took care of the whole family—and even made house calls. He may not have had as much to offer as his modern counter-part—but he was a lot more comfortable!

Today's advanced technology sometimes seems to work against the mature person's comfort level. Unfortunately, this high tech comes at a time in life when the patient needs personalized attention.

Furthermore, medical care is now problem-oriented. A woman is "a uterus," "a gall bladder." Being defined as a *condition* is demoralizing. "We have lived lives," comments Barrie Ryan. "It is hard to be seen as this other thing, the problem. A younger woman can accept being defined as a uterus without feeling a loss of identity. If you haven't lived, you can say, 'Okay, I'll accept that.' But older people want to be recognized for their struggles and achievements, not just seen as aging bodies."

When actress Kate Maxwell dressed for a rehearsal one night, she wore a tattered sweater and a very old skirt because she knew she would end up on the floor during one of the scenes. When she put on the skirt, a button popped and she pinned the waistband together with a safety pin. On the way to the theatre, her car was hit from behind. Kate was rushed to the hospital in an ambulance. Ushered into the emergency room on a stretcher, Kate discovered that in her old clothes she was considered "a nobody—just a sixty-year-old body." This is every older person's fear—to be stereotyped in a negative way and receive health care that reflects this discount.

"What do you expect at your age?" is commonly heard from physicians. The answer ought to be, "I expect to feel as good as I possibly can, and to enjoy the rest of my life."

The Physician's Dilemma

Older patients try the patience of their healers. Doctors like success stories. They want the tumor excised, the infection stopped, the gall bladder calmed or removed. Older people are disappointing to them because often they have chronic conditions. Not only do their various health conditions tend to go on and on, but they pile up and begin to interact with each other. Their medications may affect each other, too. And frankly, some older patients are not always easy to work with. Those who have not adjusted to their health problems may be angry and argumentative. Older patients may object to treatment plans or ignore their doctors' advice. They are supersensitive about being brushed aside. They speak of their doctors' negative attitudes, their preoccupation with all that is abnormal in the individual, not what is doing well. Sometimes it seems that the direction of older people and the direction of modern medicine are opposite paths.

How You Can Help Your Doctor

Men and women who are over fifty grew up in a time when the doctor was a figure of authority to be obeyed without question. People now realize the need to take more responsibility for their own health. A passive attitude is not in their best interests in today's health care system.

The patient has a responsibility to supply information and ask questions. This is especially important today, when people tend to consult a variety of specialists. No single physician may have the full picture.

Every patient should have a list of all medications he or she is taking. The list should be brought to each and every medical and dental appointment. A doctor *must* have *all* the information. To say, "I'm taking a pink pill and a long white one" will not do! Provide actual brand names and dosages, or bring the bottles with you. Be sure the doctor sees your list before prescribing more medication.

The doctor's first questions will be about your "chief complaint." Vagueness and inaccuracies make the doctor's job frustrating and difficult. Before the appointment, focus on your symptoms. Be prepared to tell the details—when the symptoms arise and how long they last. Decide what you want from this appointment with the doctor. Do you want immediate relief? A more thorough investigation? More information? As in any other situation, you are more likely to get what you want if you keep in mind what that is.

Make a written list of everything ahead of the actual visit—your symptoms, medications, any side effects, and related information. Be sure to take the list with you to the doctor's office! Many people find it helpful also to take along a relative or a friend who can provide a second voice.

If the doctor gives you a prescription, discuss the medication. Ask questions about anticipated reactions and interactions with other drugs. Report any changes in your mental or physical condition after starting on a new drug. Physicians are not mind readers; expecting them to be can be risky.

Doctors sometimes complain that their older patients ramble on, and they impatiently wonder how to stop the rambling. It is easier to stay focused if you are prepared, and you will get your needs met. You want the doctor to be aware of you as a person, true; but this is not the time to bend your doctor's ear. If you tend to use the doctor as a sounding board, perhaps you need to find other people to share your ideas with. Make the best use of your doctor by staying focused, giving all possible information, and listening carefully.

As we grow older, our physicians seem to be getting younger. It's important to remember that this is not your son or daughter sitting across the desk, but a person who is trained in medicine and whose knowledge may be more current in some areas than that of the older doctors. In any case, the young doctor deserves the same respect as the older counterpart. Telling the young doctor "what's what" can be self-defeating.

One young doctor told me how discouraged he was when he first opened his practice. He had worked hard to develop skill in treating aging patients. When he began work in his chosen field, some of his patients treated him as if he were "just a kid." This was very hard for the conscientious new professional to handle. Middle-aged and older patients need to pause, throw away their mental image of a child, and give the young professional a chance.

Young physicians may need a little breaking in, too. They may value athletic ability, independence, all the qualities that their older patients are short on; but exposure to vital, intelligent older people will help to change their perspective.

Overdose

When Doris Reed was eighty, she became ill with kidney stones. She also had pneumonia, so she had a chest doctor as well as a kidney specialist. At the hospital she was treated with a laser and a combination of antibiotics and other medications. She believes that her specialists did not compare notes and that they gave her medicines that are toxic in combination. When Doris became weak and couldn't seem to remember anything, her son looked up the drugs in *The Physician's Desk Reference* (PDR). Then he spoke to the doctor about the side effects he had read about. "My mother was sharp as a tack when she came in here," he said, "and now she doesn't know her own name." The physician said he couldn't discontinue the drugs, but the son insisted. Doris regained her memory and, she believes, her life.

Older people tend to be more sensitive to medications, and often they need lower dosages. Going to a gerontologist—a doctor who specializes in treating older people— would be a way of ensuring that the dosage is right. Or the patient can be alert to possible side effects and be reminded of how important it is to report them to the physician. People often neglect to do this. They expect physicians to have all the answers, but they fail to ask the necessary questions.

Wouldn't It Be Lovely . . .

The demands on a physician's time are many, and it is unrealistic to expect a big change. That doesn't mean we can't dream. How about going into a clinic that is warm with plants, paintings, and soothing music? When you meet with your doctor, you are dressed in your street clothes. You talk together as equal adults. The doctor seems interested in your life, with its particular struggles and achievements. The doctor writes on your chart—not "Doris Reed, eighty-four-year-old obese female with kidney stones," but "Doris Reed, former New York showgirl, now a painter and poet. Her favorite poem is Robert Frost's 'The Road Not Taken.' Doris has a few regrets about the roads she has not taken."

The examining room also is pleasant, and it is not too cold. After the examination, the physician leaves briefly so you can exchange the paper dress for street clothes. Again you talk, adult to adult, about your condition. If medication is needed, the doctor is available for further consultation about your reactions.

If tests, further procedures, or surgery are recommended, the doctor gives you the information you need in order to make an informed decision. If you decide against the recommendation, the physician will not dismiss you as a patient, but will look with you at alternative treatments. If you decide to go ahead with the surgery, the doctor is glad to know that you like Chopin and promises to play his concerti during your operation.

Medical Information Centers

A doctor told Marie that her arthritic hands could be mended with surgery. Marie checked with patients who had had the surgery, and found that their hands were bound up for a year. After the unbinding, extensive physical therapy was needed to restore functioning. Marie realized that she was better off without the surgery—at least for now, while she still has function.

An information center could help people make decisions about recommended treatments. The results of medical research could be made available, with counselors to help you to understand it.

Much of this information is already available in libraries. In the book, *Current Therapy*, therapies are outlined for all common conditions. *The Physician's Desk Reference* lists drugs, their actions, contraindications, and any adverse reactions. Medical dictionaries define the terminology. A reference titled *Index Medicus* lists recent articles on medical and psychiatric subjects. Medical libraries are another source of extensive research. You don't have to be a physician to enter; they don't search for stethoscopes at the front door.

MENTAL HEALTH CARE

Is it possible that current psychotherapeutic methods are geared for the young? Ken Dychtwald told an interviewer writing *Special Reports* that he believes they are. "Therapists often don't understand the problems of the seventy-, eighty-, and ninety-year-old, and therefore may misdiagnose them." The same might be said of therapy for the fifty- and sixty-year-old.

Like the physician, the traditional psychotherapist takes a patient history. For most clients, the family background and education become the history; then it's on to the present problem. For a sixty-year-old, there is a vast in-between area that needs to be explored.

Only 4 percent of patients in a typical psychiatric clinic are over age sixty-five. Yet depression is common in this group, especially when chronic health problems are involved. There is some evidence that the symptoms of depression may be different in older people than they are in younger patients. There seem to be more lassitude, physical complaints, and memory loss, and less anger and guilt. There is obviously quite a bit that we as an aging society need to know about emotional illness and aging.

One thing we *do* know is that people in late middle age and older can change. They are not as inflexible as we formerly thought, and most have been able to improve with therapy.

Rose Tennant, M.D., says that the pain that causes emotional stress often has been buried for years. "Older people have more years of memory accumulation to get through," says Dr. Tennant. "A lot of that has been negative, and it's necessary to drain that off. It's going to take a longer time, and a lot of older people are not willing to spend that time. But even with short-term therapy, they can be helped. They can get rid of a lot of surface emotion and learn to see things differently."

Is the reviewing of past hurts and angers likely to create a problem in itself? Dr. Tennant says not, because she takes patients through the process very slowly. "It is important to let go of the past, the buried emotions that you have put so much energy into suppressing. The release frees you to live in the present."

When is it too late to change? Never! With or without psychotherapy, it is possible to grow until the last moment of life. You may have a hornet's nest of old hurts inside, but the pain can be released and let go. Authentic living is in the present moment!

Tips on Finding a Therapist

Often a person has to try several psychotherapists to get the right one. Out of this search comes the emotional support that is such a vital part of the therapist-client relationship.

1. Sometimes friends can give a recommendation. This is not always possible, since many people do not wish to divulge that they are in therapy. Find several possible therapists through friends, clergy, professional associations, or the Yellow Pages.
2. A telephone call may tell you whether or not the various therapists you are considering have any special interest and experience in your type of problem.
3. Ask for a brief consultation to meet with the therapist before deciding to go ahead with the therapy. Most therapists don't charge for this interview. Meet several therapists before deciding to continue with one.
4. Does the prospective therapist seem compatible? Would you enjoy him or her as a personal friend if the situation were different?
5. How much does the therapist charge, and is the rate variable? Is the therapist eligible for third-party payments? If the rate is high, does the therapist conduct groups at lower fees?
6. What kind of an approach does the therapist favor: insight, cognitive, or some other technique? You may not know which type you want, but the conversation might help you know what to expect.

Things to Watch for

Good feelings between therapist and client are essential, so be alert to possible negative ones. This is hard to analyze, but often people form immediate impressions about each other. It might be well to follow your hunches in that regard.

The age and the sex of the therapist are not as important

as the feeling of relatedness. However, if you have strong preferences, now is the time to think about it.

Does Your Therapist Think You're Old?   How do you know when a therapist is fitting you into some niche called "old"? Here are a few clues.

Does the therapist seem accepting of you? Do you feel that you are being stereotyped as an older person, or does the therapist explore to find your uniqueness? Do you feel prejudged because of your gray hair? This is not to say that you should find an older therapist. Young therapists may be more in tune with a woman's need to branch out in new areas.

Another clue: Has the therapist ever referred to your sex life in the past tense, without your having done so first? A fifty-five-year-old woman was in a group therapy session, listening to the dialogue between a husband and wife about their sexual problems. Turning to the older woman, the therapist said, "I guess you remember how the sexual experience was." He seemed to fear that she would be shocked by the detailed discussion!

Has the therapist ever suggested that you are neurotic not to fall into the conventional feminine role? ("Why don't you cook breakfast for your husband?") Do you sense that the therapist thinks there isn't much use working on problems "at your age"? If so, *do not make another appointment!*

What Older Women Want
Their Therapists to Understand

1. *A pile-up of crises and losses is normal.* On the first visit to the psychotherapist, a woman lists her problems—divorce, health losses, a retarded grandchild, death of parents and friends, and difficulty in adjusting to a new

community. The therapist might assume this to be a pathological amount of problems. Yet the "normal," certainly productive, women I talked with all led lives filled with a myriad of problems.

2. *Acute distress is normal.* Anyone with a pile-up of losses eventually will become acutely distressed. If not, it would be a sign of unreality.

Actress Kate Maxwell saw a psychiatrist when she returned from Mexico to find that her house had been sold, her husband had found a younger woman, she had no money and no career, she was getting too old to play most leading roles, and she had no one to talk to. "Everything in the world is hitting me," she told the psychiatrist. She cried and talked about her losses. Suddenly the psychiatrist asked, "Who is the President of the United States? What's the name of his dog? What's the name of the street out front?" Kate realized that the doctor was judging her competence. Kate thought, "I'd better not be incompetent; I have to support myself," and she left the office. The reason she felt as if everything in the world was hitting her was because it was!

3. *Don't be overwhelmed by our losses.* A therapist could pick up on all these calamities and think that the case is beyond help. But part of growing older is accepting loss, letting go, and finding new connections. Mature people are able to do this, especially if they have some emotional support and guidance.

There is no "hopeless case." Elisabeth Kübler-Ross described a seventy-year-old woman who was depressed and terminally ill. The patient said she had made all the wrong decisions in her life, had failed at everything, and that her life had come to nothing. Kübler-Ross responded by asking the woman to tell what she had learned from her experiences so that it might be of benefit to others. The patient did so, and in the process she became involved with other patients and the hospital staff. A few days before she died, the woman said, "These have been the best nine months of my life."

4. *Recognize our strengths.* How have we come this far? We have survived! We have lived through enough societal changes and expectations to challenge several lifetimes, enough problems to fill a book. We have some solid coping abilities, and these can be drawn on for further adaptation.

5. *I'm not your mother.* There is a risk that the older woman will remind a therapist of his or her mother—not a good situation because many younger people have unresolved issues with their mothers. It is essential for the therapist to keep personal issues out of the treatment situation. Fortunately, there are therapists of all ages who are free from this kind of entanglement.

   On the other hand, your task is not to *be* a mother! Avoid commenting, "when I was your age" or "my daughter has an outfit like that." Realize that the therapist may not have the benefit of your experience, but *does* have the knowledge and understanding to help you.

6. *We're not too old to grow and change.* We are interested in forming better relationships and finding new directions in life, and we desire all the things that younger people desire.

CHAPTER TEN

Reclaiming Our Heritage

Today's woman, according to the TV commercials, is more at home in the boardroom than over the scrub board. She drives home to perform fifteen-minute miracles with pasta and shrimp, corrals the children to their homework and baths, and then settles down with a glass of Chardonnay for a romantic evening with her husband. This is the life, far more glamorous than women in previous generations could enjoy. Then why isn't she happier?

In reality, today's woman may have learned to be aggressive, to play the game, but many times she feels cheated. Instinctively she knows there is something false about the cutthroat competition, the long hours of work, the pressure. Is this why she got an M.B.A.—to achieve this kind of bogus power? Arriving home exhausted, she pops a frozen dinner in the microwave and struggles through the dinner and bedtime routine with the children. Most evenings she isn't up to playing seductress to her husband. She wonders why he doesn't help out more.

This is paradise compared to what can come later. At fifty, the wife has a few wrinkles and gray hairs, and she feels neglected. Adult children move away, anxious to take charge of their own lives. Advice from Mother is regarded as meddlesome, not helpful, and contacts with her are relegated to a few telephone calls and frantic holiday reunions. She may be in the boardroom—or she may be out of a job. The "old boy network" still prevails. No matter hard she works as executive and mother, she somehow feels left in the lurch.

Something is wrong. We find some clues in studying the ancient cultures, which feature women as important and wise.

WHERE WRINKLES MEAN POWER AND INFLUENCE

We pity the peasant women in undeveloped parts of the world; they have no amenities at all. None at all? That's not quite true. Actually, anthropologists have discovered that women with wrinkles and some years have much influence and prestige in most Third World societies. They gain status as they age, at least in the traditional concepts of those cultures. Of course, we don't want to live like the !Kung women in Africa, grinding corn with stones and losing their teeth. But their lives are freer, simpler than yours and mine. Not only does their social status improve with age, but their freedom in sexual behavior eases as well. Instead of designer dresses, these women wear primitive pubic aprons. As the years go by, they are permitted to drop their aprons lower and lower, until not much of anything is covered. This new freedom is not confined to the

!Kung, but is found in many primitive tribes. !Kung women may be poor, they'll never see Bermuda, but they do have fun!

In most preindustrial cultures, aging women are on the rise in terms of aggression and power. In no culture did the anthropologists find that the men had increasing authority over their wives. They found several trends in most of the cultures they studied:

1. With advancing age, the woman begins to be the dominant person in the home, often sharing the authority with her eldest son.
2. The woman retains some control over her sons and their wives, and in this way she preserves her territory. She is the advisor, the organizer, the leader of the extended family.
3. At menopause, the woman becomes acceptable in sacred places and she takes on ritualistic tasks. In many cultures, women are healers as well purveyors of the culture.

Women who reach fifty and are not accorded the power that is their tradition—perhaps because they have no sons—become morose and ill. In this respect, they are much like their counterparts in America who are unable to find a fulfilling role in life.

In some Third World societies, a woman who uses her powers in ways that upset the society will be called a witch. This happens when family tensions prevent her from the dominance in the home that is due her. The family says that she is under the influence of evil spirits.

But wise woman or witch, the older woman is seen as more potent than when she was young. Anthropologist David Gutmann proposes that the older woman's depression in our culture may be due not only to her many losses, but to the frustration of her natural aggression that surfaces at this time of life. In our culture, there is no appreciation or approved outlet for this new energy. We have ignored the growth potential of the middle-aged woman.

Western women may not care to be the administrators of a household of children and grandchildren, but they do need some kind of role and recognition for it. Obviously, this recognition will have to take a different track.

In older cultures, a woman's work in food preparation is basic to the survival of the tribe. It is honored further for its role in spiritual rituals. Ancient cultures often centered around those two events—the survival of the clan and the life of the spirit. Today, the taking of food is not held sacred but is trivialized by its easy availability. The businessman and woman may have lunch brought in by a caterer, dinner at a restaurant, and a snack from a vending machine. The children long not for Mother's pot roast but for a McDonald's quarter-pounder.

The role of medicine woman has been usurped by experts, mostly male. Attending the birth of babies, healing the sick, counseling the distressed, are no longer the areas presided over by grandmothers. An army of obstetricians, internists, psychiatrists, and other experts has taken over.

Surely, we find that older females are submissive in the animal kingdom? No! Even middle-aged monkeys do well! The young female ape devotes herself to the latest infant and allies herself to a dominant male, trading her sexual services in exchange for his protection. She is cautiously nonaggressive with other adults. But a striking change occurs when she is past the reproductive years. Suddenly, in the face of danger from other animals, she leaps to the front lines and joins the young males in combat!

There is something reassuringly primitive and biological about late-life female ascendancy. Judith Brown and Virginia Kerns' book *In Her Prime* describes this phenomenon in detail.

A CHINESE WOMAN TALKS ABOUT AGING

The honoring of age in China started in the very beginning, before the written word. People reasoned that you learn through your life experiences. It follows, then, that the wisest are those who have the most life experiences. They decided on the authority of the social unit by who was eldest. Everyone in the unit could look forward to respecting age and then being respected when his or her turn came. Confucius (551-479 B.C.) reinforced this arrangement during the Chou dynasty, when he said we should love all elderly as we love our parents and we should care for all children as we care for our own. Chinese people revere the older generations as being the treasure of the country. This is also true in Japan and many other Asian countries.

Elizabeth Lau, a Chinese-American social worker who works in a hospital in San Francisco, lived in Hong Kong for twenty-eight years before coming to America thirty-one years ago. She reflects on the elder Chinese women in her community and in her own family.

"We don't call them senior citizens. We call them Best Citizen. Kay-ying. This means the best of the better ones, the top-notch." She observes that older Chinese women are more content than their American counterparts, even if their children have moved away.

Elizabeth described a typical day in the lives of her elderly mother and aunts. "They wake up to mah-jongg," she says. "It's a game something like bridge and poker. The game begins in the morning, and it continues through the day. It's not like the American bridge scene, where players get together two or three times a week. The mah-jongg is on the table in the morning, and they spend the entire day and evening at the table, with time out to prepare and eat their meals. Sometimes the group will go out to dinner together before the evening game. They say, 'The more I play mah-jongg, the healthier I feel. . . .Only when I stop the mah-jongg game do I feel stiff. The mah-jongg can cure all disease.' This is true in the sense that it is a distraction, a pleasant and stimulating way to spend the day."

A whole day and evening of social activity might stress many Americans, who are used to more privacy and independence. But the Chinese culture involves a close interaction. People visit one another without necessarily making previous plans. You can walk into the home of a close relative or friend, and she doesn't feel she has to stop to get you a cup of coffee. She can continue to wash the clothes or cook, and you are free to follow her around, often helping out. A Chinese housewife is not lonely, like her Western counterpart. Giving a dinner party? A sister-in-law will come to the house and help with the marketing, the cooking, and the cleaning. The hostess will return the favor, interrupting her life to help the sister-in-law with her dinner the next week.

"One time," Elizabeth relates, "the plumbing at my parents' house broke down at one o'clock in the morning. A water pipe broke, and the water kept running. My parents knocked on the door of a cousin, a neighbor. Dressed in his pajamas, he came to their house, helped stop the water, stayed to talk for a couple of hours, and finally ended up sleeping there."

Children also are part of the community social life, unlike Western culture that divides people into different age groups. Everyone may spend the day together in a small living room. A mother may be knitting as her daughter does homework. The daughter might say, "I really hate this teacher. She gives us so much homework." The mother responds right then and there. The children have appreciation for the mother who takes time to talk with them. The mother, in turn, feels she has achieved and accomplished a great deal by raising her children, seeing them get married and have careers and families of their own.

It is this atmosphere of close interaction and trust, this family closeness, that forms the family structure that honors older women.

When a young Chinese woman marries, her mother tells her, "When you go to the new family, make sure you're obedient." This may sound oppressive, but less so when you realize the caring that both mothers have toward the young woman. Her mother has prepared her for this day so that she will not resent the authority. The mother-in-law is the undisputed mistress of the house. She loves the bride as her own, and gives her care and protection as well as instruction. This domination must be difficult for the young woman. It must be remembered, however, that Chinese elders have spent their lives much more in touch with their children than have their American counterparts. There have been ongoing dialogue and a long-standing atmosphere of sharing and respect. Even if the husband takes a concubine, the wife's position is not threatened because she also will be in charge of the concubine.

Elizabeth Lau believes she has managed to incorporate the best of the two cultures. She has both the fulfillment of a career and a close support system at home. She has written six books on child development and parenting. One book, *Innovative Parenting*, combines psychoanalytic findings with Chinese cultural methods of raising children. She hopes that she will be able to influence her children's and grandchildren's lives through interest and love rather than by control.

Since age brings status, the Chinese woman doesn't fear wrinkles. Her appearance had already changed many years before. As an unmarried girl she wore her hair long, often in pigtails. When she married she bundled up her hair in the traditional manner. She toned down the colors in her clothing, and she seldom wore makeup. She did these things to show her loyalty and devotion to her family.

Now older, she has no reason for an identity crisis. She already has her gratification in her family, her applause in the children's appreciation, her pride in the belief that she has done something important. Even if her children have moved away, she is not lonely because of the unique interaction of the community. Now she can live the rest of her days in peace and harmony. Of course, life is changing for Chinese women, but the women who are now late-middle-aged have their honor, their friends, and their mah-jongg.

THE STRENGTH OF JEWISH WOMEN

Sarah Lerner, the radiant eighty-four-year-old world traveler I met on the cruise boat, remembers generations of strong Jewish women whose strength shaped her own life. They were honored by their families, much as society now honors men as the "head of the house." It is true that in a traditional Jewish home the men are served first at dinner, but it is the woman who sits at the place of honor and lights the candles.

On the Sabbath, a song-prayer is still sung to the "Queen of the Sabbath, Queen of the House."

The sun on the treetops no longer is seen.
Come, let us welcome Shabbat, the true Queen.
Behold her descending, the holy, the blessed,
And with her God's angels of peace and of rest.
Come now, come now, our Queen, our Bride.

Friday evening family worship is a tradition in Jewish homes. The woman of the house lights the candles as songs are sung and the man of the house reads *Eishet Hayil*:

A good wife, who can find? She is precious far beyond
rubies.

Her husband trusts in her, and he shall lack nothing
thereby.

She renders him good and not evil all the days of her
life.

She opens her hands to the needy and extends her hands
to the poor.

She is robed in strength and dignity, and cheerfully
faces the future.

She opens her mouth with wisdom; her tongue is guided
by kindness.

She tends to the affairs of the household and eats not
the bread of idleness.

Her children come forward and bless her; her husband,
too, and praises her: Many women have done su-
perbly, but you surpass them all.

How glorious if every woman could receive such affirmation every Friday night, attended by her family! Individual affirmations, done in secret, pale by comparison!

Sarah Lerner's grandmother fought for women's rights.
She sent her daughter, Sarah's mother, from a country village in the Hungarian-Austrian area to Vienna to get an
education and see the broader world. The grandmother
often said to Sarah, "Be your own person first, and then get
married."

Larry, a sixty-plus therapist, recalls stories about his
grandmother, Esther. She had a tea shop in their small
village in Russia. One day, cossacks came to kill her husband. They ordered her to go get him. "Why?" she asked.
"Because he is Jewish," they replied. "I am Jewish, too,"
Esther said. "Kill *me!*" But they only shrugged. "Well, I'll tell
you," she confided, "I've wanted to get rid of that man for

years. I'll help you. Wait here. I'll bring him to you." She went to the back of the store and whispered to the maid, "Get my husband out of the house!" Her husband fled, and Esther was credited with saving his life through her cleverness and quick wit. Months later, the couple landed at Ellis Island. On the ship, Esther's husband's eyes had started to run from a cold. Anyone with eye disease would not be allowed into the United States, and Esther was afraid the immigration officials wouldn't believe he had just a common cold. She made a fuss, bombarding them with demands. Finally the officials let them in to put a stop to Esther's harangue. And so, another family got its start in America.

NATIVE AMERICAN WOMEN

There were no anthropologists back in the 1500s, and accounts we have are brief; but early English and Spanish explorers did report finding Indian chieftesses in the New World. Fernando de Soto, a Spanish explorer, came upon a powerful woman ruler in the southeast in 1540. In the same century, English explorers found an Indian queen in Virginia. When the chief was a man, often a group of older women formed a council. The Iroquois, in what is now New York state, are an Indian culture that leaned toward matriarchy. Ownership of land and responsibility to the children passed through the mother's side of the family. Cherokee women also had influence in the government of their towns. A woman's council was presided over by "Beloved Woman." Every Hopi village was headed by a matriarch, who was consulted by male relatives on family matters. The leader of the Hopi town was a man, but he consulted with a woman who held the title, "Keeper of the Fire." That woman was chosen on the basis of her wisdom and intelligence.

Women tended to be experts at collecting not only food but also herbs for medication. An older woman who developed a skill in herbal or spiritual healing could become influential. Sometimes those women learned their skills by assisting the tribal medicine man. A woman needed to have her healing powers validated by a dream in which she received knowledge from a supernatural force. The culture encouraged meditation and personal vision, and these dreams were a part of Indian experience.

Ceremonies marked the four stages of a person's life: Infant's Reception into Life; Youth's Vigil and Quest of Vision; the adult's Self-Proof and Recognition; and the older person's years of reflection, Memory and Passing. Each stage of life was seen as fraught with peril. An older person was honored not only for whatever wisdom they may have personally attained, but also for the spiritual strength that brought them that far.

"The Voice of a Woman": Jean Chaudhuri's Story

Jean Chaudhuri grew up in a traditional culture as a Creek Indian in Oklahoma. Listening to Jean in her Tempe, Arizona, home, I became aware that Indian women are trained for influence from the time they are young. Jean speaks from experience, as one who has reached the age of contemplation; yet her face is young and unlined, her eyes bright and determined.

When Jean and her sister were young girls, their mother gave them lessons in breathing and singing. They were taught to project their voices effectively and make forceful presentations, yet be silent and thoughtful when others wished to speak. Today Jean's full, strong voice reflects the energy that lies within. Indian women are no longer given this traditional training, but many Indian women she knows try to emulate her so they, too, can have "the voice of a woman" and influence their community.

Jean and her sister learned about life and about their traditions outside, in the shade of the ramada. They were told the story of the four seasons of life. They learned of their obligations to family, clan, and community, and of the spiritual values that would make their life meaningful. They were taught to sing the songs that were important to that culture and to be involved with religion and morality.

When Jean was eight years old, hard times forced the family to give up their forty acres of rural land and move to the city. "I cried and cried," Jean said. But her father told her, "There are times when we have to leave things. There's always a transition, but we must evolve. This is only one of many evolvements that you will have."

"On the last day," Jean remembers, "I ran through the little pathways and spoke to the pecan trees. 'I won't be able to enjoy your food.' I went to the persimmons. I touched everything that was on the property I was raised on. I refused to leave this little paradise. Father said, 'Never look back. The memories will guide you. Remember what you did on this property. That will never be erased from your mind. And when you're sick or heartsick or lonesome, remember what you did.'" Her mother said gently, "Remember that the Creator has given you your identity through a language, through your ways, through your love of Mother Earth. Never forget that. Never forget who you are."

A cold wind was blowing when the family left their home at 4:00 A.M. for the two-mile walk to the bus stop. It was raining, and the cold pierced their bodies. Jean's mother lit a lantern, and as they walked through the darkness she started to sing. She told the children the story of the Trail of Tears, when the tribes had to walk from Florida to Oklahoma. "Just think," she said, "we are getting only a touch of what they had to go through." The children snuggled up to her and the lantern, which gave only a little light and no heat. "It was enough for us," Jean remembers.

In the city, Jean rebelled at learning English. Father sat down beside her. "Do you remember the times we played hand shadows on the wall and I told you stories about the different animals?" he asked. "Do you remember that the animals learned our language, and we learned to understand what they needed when they grunted? When we did that, we learned to understand their way of life.

"Remember this," he continued. "A person who knows two languages, who understands two ways of life and knows that there are different people, will be as valuable as *two* people. This is what you must do now."

Her father was a storyteller, a member of the bird clan noted for the ability to communicate. She learned from him the importance of being alone to think, and to join with others to make a better world. Jean's family is a matriarchy, so she follows her mother's clan, the bear, noted for abilities in herbal medicine and oratory. How fortunate every woman would be to have Jean's father and mother as teachers of wisdom!

As a young woman Jean had a mentor, a Sioux Indian woman, Ella Deloria, the first woman Indian anthropologist. She was eighty-five years old when Jean was twenty-seven. Ella had a deep appreciation of cultural differences, and she guided Jean in developing her appreciation of other cultures. "She opened my eyes," Jean relates. Jean had five mentors in all, each helping her as she passed through a different stage of life.

In the traditional Indian culture, the women analyzed the agricultural needs of the community, then formulated plans to achieve the desired ends. The men had input in the planning and were in charge of carrying out the plans.

Creek women were taught that it is important to be a part of the system. They also were taught to speak to the issue if they saw injustice.

Jean's father told her she could do anything she wanted to do, and he reminded her that she had many options. Jean worked hard in the 1970s to get a free election for her tribe. She began to understand political pressure, how laws are made, how to present bills. Eventually, Jean became executive director of the Indian Center in Tucson. She organized an open-door clinic for the poor from nearby reservations. She also has worked on educational services for Native American children, and she has campaigned to have more input in community government.

In 1977, Jean was one of five people in the nation to win the Jefferson Award from the American Institute of Public Service. Today she is sharing her knowledge and experience by writing articles, plays, and a book about the four seasons of life. The training of her people, the wisdom of her parents, and the presence of mentors, all had important roles in the development of this woman who "speaks with a woman's voice."

ANCIENT GODDESSES

A young man bent down, pressed a stick into the moist clay, and began to draw symbols. It was the first formal writing. Were the symbols in praise of the Queen of Heaven, the Great Goddess, the Supreme Creator?

It seemed natural to worship a woman in this dawn of society. Women cultivated the fields and organized a steady food supply. This permitted the tribal members to abandon the earlier nomadic hunting life, build villages close to the fields, and establish a social system. Furthermore, those early people viewed women as the bearers of life. Scientists had not yet evolved to tell us that the male sperm also activates human life. All these people knew was that they were born and they died. The female's obvious involvement in birth was a powerful message that inspired awe and respect. They also saw the woman's devotion to her children, and that love was likened to the divine love of a Creator.

Those "heathen idol worshippers" the Bible refers to were praying to a female goddess. Queen of Heaven, Innin, Inanna, Nana, Anahita, Istar, Isis, Asherah, were some of her names. Some archaeologists trace the female deity back to 25,000 B.C., thousands of years before Abraham, the first prophet of the male deity Yahweh.

These goddesses were not sentimentalized madonnas who were loved for their gentle, nurturing abilities. They had distinct qualities that today we think of as "male." They invented language, began agriculture, and were known for their capacity to think and reason. In Ireland, Cirriden was the goddess of knowledge and intelligence. Maat, in Egypt, created the order, rhythm, and truth of the universe. In Greece, Demeter dealt with the law, dispensing wisdom and justice. Other goddesses brought spiritual insights to the people. All of them had power, wisdom, and strength.

What happened? Historical research is hampered by the fact that the use of letters did not describe human experience until well after 2000 B.C. This coincided with the arrival of assorted invaders from the north who brought their patriarchal gods and set about to undermine and finally destroy the female goddesses. Merlin Stone, in her extraordinary book, *When God Was a Woman*, described the archaeological evidence of these goddesses from many cultures.

In the early societies that worshipped goddesses, the same reasoning about women being the source of life resulted in mother-kin societies. They were matrilineal; that is, property was inherited through the females. A man acquired property only as he was related to a woman as her son or husband. A woman had status not necessarily as a political head but as the bearer of life and the provider of wealth.

The Women of Ancient Egypt

The great centers of culture moved gradually from the Eastern Mediterranean area west to Europe. In grade school, we learned about the pharaohs and the pyramids of Egypt. What we didn't learn about Egypt was that in prehistoric times the goddess held supremacy. In Northern Egypt she was called Nekhebt and in Southern Egypt she was called Nut, Net, or Nit. When nothing else had been created, she created all life. It was she who placed Ra, the sun-god, in the sky. Later, Isis incorporated and eventually replaced Nut.

Is it possible that societies that worshipped women also gave them more economic or political prestige? Which came first, the goddess or the prestige? We do not know. What we *do* know is that ancient Egyptian women had great freedom and control over their lives. In the fifth century B.C., Herodotus wrote, "Women go into the marketplace, transact affairs, and occupy themselves with business, while the husbands stay home and weave." Love poems discovered in Egyptian tombs strongly hint that women took the initiative in courting. But by 1500 B.C., the role of the women and the goddess had declined.

Crete and the High Priestess

Archaeological research at the temple of Knossos in Crete reveals information about a high priestess who represented the Great Goddess on earth during the Minoan civi-

lization (3000 B.C.-1100 B.C.). The society was matri-
archal, with powerful women controlling the wealth. During
the classical age of Greece that we all studied about in
school, about 500-200 B.C., Northern influences brought
patriarchy to Greece. Worship passed then to the god Zeus,
who later became Jupiter in Rome.

What could have happened to overthrow the worship of
the female principal, the Great Goddess, and so completely
reverse religious and social thinking? Perhaps someone figured out that life was not created by women alone, that the
male provider of sperm also was involved. Or perhaps it was
all due to the northern tribes who invaded the more established cultures to the south. In a series of migrations that
took place over several thousand years, beginning about
2400 B.C., these invaders appeared as groups of warriors to
conquer the older settlements, and they were followed by
their priests bringing their own gods.

The invaders also brought with them their concepts of
light as good and dark as evil. Coming from the north,
perhaps the light seemed especially precious to them. They
didn't throw over the goddesses immediately, but they rein-
terpreted them. The female deity came to be associated
with the serpent and with darkness and evil powers. The
male deity was always the champion of light. The ground-
work was being laid for the worship of the Hebrew god
Yahweh.

The goddess was not completely forgotten, however.
The Egyptian goddess Maat remained, but she changed with
the times. As the deity in charge of order in the universe
and all that is good, she was allowed to stay on—provided
she attached herself to a male deity. Law and order still
could be maintained by Maat as long as she could be con-
trolled by the king. She represented a strange duality—the
ultimate wisdom and an ominous, underlying chaos.

The temple of Isis in Ephesus, seen by many tourists,

was in use—but in a diminished way—as late as 465 B.C.,
not long before the birth of Christ.

CAN WE REGAIN SOME OF OUR POWER?

Some researchers believe that this radical shift in religion and culture created the social and political problems that women have today. Perhaps by recalling the ancient ways of honoring women in past cultures, women can regain their lost power. There's no need to start building temples to Isis, but women do need to be recognized for their experience and the wisdom they have attained.

The spiritual world as well as the secular world needs the contribution of women. While today's spiritual leaders tend to be men, this, too, is beginning to change. Women often say, "Now that I know so much, nobody wants to hear about it." Yet many women are finding ways to make their ideas heard. They are beginning to find their voice.

CHAPTER ELEVEN

Reflections

ON MONEY AND POWER

"Society went off track when it started ignoring religion and worshipping money and power," says Doris Reed. "You see it everywhere. Remember that company that watered down their apple juice? Imagine doing that to save a couple of pennies! One company brought out apple juice that contained no apple juice at all!

"Along with amassing money, people want to have a good time. Life isn't having a good time. Life is sacrificing for somebody. If someone you love is ill, you nearly kill yourself to get them well. It isn't money. Look at Mrs. Marcos with her hundreds of shoes, poor deluded woman.

"In today's materialistic society," Doris continues, "the profit motive has exploded into greed. Forgotten is human welfare, character, the things that in the long run really matter.

"I feel sorry for the younger generation, with their material possessions and no babies," says Doris. "I can imagine the funeral procession when they die. There won't be many people—no children, no grandchildren. You know how people tie tin cans on the back of wedding cars? I have a vision of a hearse with a lot of material junk tied to the back!"

ON CHILDREN

Sitting across from a portrait she painted of her daughter, Doris speaks about the present life of children in our culture. "Children are deprived," she says. "They used to have rabbits and flowers and birds. Now what does a child see, holding onto Mother's hand at the shopping mall? Rumps, pocketbooks, and feet! It's no wonder that shopping makes them irritable and stressed out.

"'Give me a penny, give me a penny!' Children run to Mother, then back to the chewing gum machine that caught their eye. 'I want this' and 'I want that.' They have no real joy. They don't have the opportunity to chase butterflies, watch birds, enjoy having a bunny in their arms. They are deprived of the chance to develop slowly in their own ways."

ON HAPPINESS

Philosopher and theologian Dennis Praeger writes, "Our society has confused fun and happiness. Even when party after party, lover after lover, drink after drink, fail to produce happiness, they keep going back for more. If these activities created happiness, it would follow that a seductive alcoholic, going to continuous parties, would be the happiest person on earth."

Real happiness is more likely to be the result of less egocentric endeavors that are not often very much fun and may even cause pain. Raising children is a prime example. Couples who have decided not to have children are spared many difficulties, but they will never know the deep satisfaction of seeing their child develop.

My neighbor, an older physician, watches as his son and daughter-in-law redecorate their large home and plan a cruise around the world. They have chosen not to spend their energies on a family. "They don't know what life is all about," comments the doctor sadly.

ON SEX AS TRIVIAL PURSUIT

Women expressed fear that the new sexual freedom increases society's trend to treat women as objects, not as human beings. Carla Whitcomb's daughters are grown. "Today's young women don't value themselves enough," she believes. "They are unaware of the enormity of the sexual relationship. Without emotional investment, what is that sexual relationship? It is nothing but Trivial Pursuit.

"We were told, 'If a man can get free milk, why should he buy the cow?' Young women disdain this saying, but older women see the younger ones as losing out on a chance for a sustaining kind of love."

ON CONTINUED LEARNING

Sarah Lerner, who continued to take university classes until well into her seventies, feels a little sad about the system of teacher assigning material and student reporting back and taking an examination. Sarah has a great love of learning. Finally, she told one professor, "I am tired of proving to you that I have read certain books. You can be sure that if they are worthwhile, I will read them." She continues to learn, but not usually in a formal classroom.

"We should take a look at the assumption that learning means endless college degrees," Sarah believes. "Some vital kinds of learning are out there in the world, in the experiences and accumulated knowledge of many people. University learning is insular, narrowing. It fits in with our present society's mood, that of specialization; but is it true learning?"

Society needs the insight of generalists, people who see the big picture and can put things together in a more creative way. Grandmothers are a group of generalists, who might enjoy more influence in society if this fact were appreciated.

ON GETTING IT ALL TOGETHER

There are two special strategies that help late-middle-aged and older people to get to know their true selves and make sense of their lives. These methods do not involve therapists, and they require little or no expense. Both involve writing one's impressions of the world.

The First Method: Journal Writing

A flood of feelings, thoughts, states of mind, memories, and ideas passes constantly through the conscious mind. One moment we see the them clearly, and the next moment they are gone. Yet they are the contents of the process of inner development. Inner growth is irregular, elusive. Even when something important is emerging, a person may be misled by despair into thinking that no growth is taking place. It was this observation that led psychologist Ira Progoff to explore journal writing as a tool for growth.

Through the process of writing down some of our fleeting thoughts and emotions, we capture them. Thus, we can better observe our inner lives, our own inner growth. Over time, the journal entries show us what our various impressions were *for*—what their purpose was in our lives. We gradually discover that our lives are moving in a definite direction. A connective thread is forming beneath the surface. We learn that the peaks and valleys are of equal importance in our growth; life emerges, revealing its purpose and goal. At the same time, self-understanding expands and gives strength and wisdom to this growth.

Ira Progoff published his journal-writing techniques and presents his methods in workshop classes under the trademark, Intensive Journal. Although it is possible to purchase Progoff's book and proceed alone, he recommends that you begin with a workshop. The group provides incentive and support, and the members share some of their entries with each other. It is not necessary to have a particular writing skill or special education. In fact, sometimes professional writers get carried away with their words and go in circles instead of going with the flow. Journal writing does unleash creativity, however.

Carla Whitcomb has been writing in a journal for many years. She bought a steno pad, started to write, and never stopped. She is now on volume 17. Retired university teacher Ruth Gardner starts each day by writing in her journal. She is interested in Jung's concept of the integration and insight possible at this time in life. Having given up the structure and purpose that was part of her working life, she finds that through the journal she is evolving the kind of life she wants now.

"The Gifts of Age"   Barrie Ryan brings a modified form of the journal workshop to seniors in Tucson. As an English instructor at a community college, Barrie realized that her courses didn't really meet the needs of her older students.

They wanted to know not just what the famous authors wrote, but also how to assimilate those experiences in their own lives. Barrie developed the Gifts of Age, a journal-writing course in which people discuss the issues of growing older. Emphasis is on the positive, spiritual side of life, but the negative aspects are attended to as well. Her students range in age from fifty-five to eighty-two. All are struggling with their identity, often after the death of a spouse.

Barrie assigns books by May Sarton and other women who saw that aging can bring enlightenment. There are lighthearted stories and essays as well. Her students bring notebooks, write about relevant subjects that reflect their own thoughts and experiences, and share their entries. Specific journal entries are assigned as homework.

One of her students told Barrie, "There is nowhere else we can talk about these things with each other. Oh, there are social situations, and clinical situations like group therapy, and support groups based on a particular interest—but where are the situations that allow us to explore and share our experiences and impressions of daily life!"

The beauty and power of the class was in the support the men and women experienced among one another. When the class ended, the members continued to meet informally.

Although Barrie's class is unique, it would not be difficult to duplicate. Barrie cannot be everywhere; but every community has many people who could lead this kind of journal-writing group. The modified journal writing group, as well as the traditional one, is a special way of bringing support and insight.

The Second Method: Life Review

More deliberate than the journal writing of daily impressions is the studied, comprehensive effort to write a "life review."

As we grow older, the events of our lives seem to flash before us as if we were the proverbial drowning man. You may want to write about them. Recording the events of your life can bring forth greater insight and understanding of how it all fits together, what it has meant. This exercise, however, is not one to be undertaken in desperation. A person deep in regrets and fears about the past may not find this a nourishing process. The life review might best be undertaken in a therapy situation or in a writing group made up of people who are writing their autobiographies. The support and sharing of a group may make the difference between being upset or uplifted. Some people tend to recall only life's unpleasant moments. It might be a good preliminary exercise to go over the events of one's life, focusing on the pleasures and writing about them, before beginning to write about the many other facets of one's life.

What a wonderful gift it would be for children and grandchildren if everyone wrote an autobiography! Not every writer has such a ready-made audience! By writing not just, "I got married in 1949" but by telling about one's courtship and early married life, you can pass down the gift of who you are!

ON *REAL* OLD AGE:
THE PAINFUL LOOK AHEAD

Women seem to panic more at the thought of old age than they do at the thought of death. To be elderly and ill is such a horror that people don't want to think about it. They are afraid of being dependent, reduced to the indignity of incapacity. It is difficult even to talk about old age because of its connotation of physical and mental breakdown. Yet, statistically, only 5 percent of the elderly end up in nursing homes.

Doris Reed, looking younger than eighty-four, is alert and articulate. Yet she told me, "I didn't believe I was going to be old. I was going to be young until I died, like a butterfly. . . . The plums are falling off the tree. Aging is a circle that closes. Everything goes—your looks, your memory, your ability to drive. Everything isn't going to get better; it's going to get worse. I saw a lady get up from a chair, and the chair was wet. Age is embarrassing. I feel so depleted from what I was. Once I put a box of graham crackers in the refrigerator, and then I started looking around for them. I expected other people to treat me as if I were stupid, but just the opposite has happened. People are very nice to me. Children jump up and open doors for me— a happy surprise."

Ruth Gardner had a great model for aging—her mother, who remained in love with life until the end. When Ruth studied Shakespeare, her mother read, too, and Shakespeare became her favorite author. When she died suddenly, Ruth found her mother's textbooks and lecture notes on a course in Hindu philosophy.

Ruth talked with me about a book she read recently on the subject of aging. It is *The Measure of My Days*, by Florida Scott-Maxwell. The author writes that she believes the eightieth decade is the best, because all exterior things are gone. Friends are gone, distractions are gone. You are back with existence, the way you are as a child. This time it is different, because the years between have changed your perspective in "being."

Acceptance of the end of life seems easier than the submission to old age. A few women I talked with look forward to it as a kind of release. Others do not; yet they see death as a natural happening and nothing to fear.

Ruth, who believes in a new life after death, thinks death is an interesting concept. "If I were in charge of a universe and had to think of a way to end it all, when it's so fantastic, I would have a great unknown. There is more here than anybody can accomplish or do. There is more than we can see in a lifetime. What could possibly be more dramatic and keep everyone's interest than an ending that is unknown? Life has built-in suspense. Death may be an exciting climax to this whole adventure."

BUT IN THE MEANTIME . . .

We can't just wait around for our society to shape up and honor older people. We can concentrate on what we can do.

1. Recognize that this is a different stage of life, no matter how young you look and feel, so you need to get prepared. It's great to still feel young, but society sees you as one who is growing older. There is still time to make plans.

2. You need a new strategy, a new life purpose, to meet the new challenge. When you are in your fifties is the best time to start, but the sixties and seventies are "better late than never." The gains you make earlier will prevent a more serious crisis later in life.

3. Separate your self-image from the distorted image that society has of anyone over fifty, lest you incorporate it and feel defeated.

4. You live in society, so take every opportunity to use its resources and opportunities as you plan your new horizons. Make use of vocational counseling, therapy, journal writing—whatever you think will help you learn.

5. Once you have found your new life purpose, take the important step of following through with *action*. Take a risk! Don't worry so much about what happens next! The gap between wishing and succeeding is the actual *doing*.

6. If your goal is paid employment, spend time on education and volunteer work in your profession. Or consider counseling and education to find a new career, regardless of your age. Don't let anyone tell you that late middle age is too late to start. Keep in mind that learning is still not only possible but may be accelerated because of your experience and motivation.

   Avoid taking a low-level job, even at a volunteer level. Once hired, a woman over fifty is not likely to work her way up. Enter at as high a level as you can. Consider starting your own business if you have the stamina and drive to carry it through.

   If you are already employed, don't fear changes on the job. Older people know that some of the new changes won't work; they've seen them tried before. But younger bosses don't want to hear about it, and that is frustrating. A more threatening problem is the new technology of the workplace. Computers may seem intimidating at first. Learning to operate them may take a bit more time than for younger workers, but it is important to stay calm and assure others that you are willing to learn the new techniques. Younger workers also fear and resent changes. They are less apt to show their uneasiness, however, perhaps feeling they can always get a new job if this doesn't work out.

7. Remember that living is your major career. You can meet your need for personal growth in creative, spiritual, and community activities. "Living" can be thought of in its larger sense: growing emotionally, having loving relationships, and being useful in the world. Working it all out is the challenge people face in a world that sometimes thinks we should "throw in the towel" and sit out the rest of our lives in the rocking chair.

8. If the long focus on the children and your husband's job has kept you from resolving basic issues, get counsel-

ing. Marriages have to be "renegotiated," in a sense, to keep up with changing times. In the traditional marriage, says Rachel Zane, a woman is willing to overlook many things. Husbands and children may demand a lot of services "because you love us." Many women get trapped in this waiting-on-others kind of life, all under the guise of love. Things could get worse when your husband retires. If he hasn't thought about his own life, he may want you to somehow work it out for him. If you're not careful, this may involve greatly increased supportive services from you.

If you are single, don't despair. Women alone are not burdened with these expectations, and they are at an advantage when they branch out in new directions. Most of the women I talked with who now find their lives successful and meaningful are widowed or divorced. Several said that to marry an older man would tie them down. "Along with the role of wife," they say, "the role of nurse is the unspoken part of the job description."

9. Learn ways of caring for your health and preventing serious problems. If you do have a health problem, be aware that it is usually possible to be sick and well at the same time. It is the inner feeling of well-being that makes the good life possible—not an official clearance from pathology. Find health care providers that you can talk to and feel comfortable with. One over-fifty group suggests that members make a list of physicians, dentists, opticians, physical therapists, psychotherapists, who have been especially caring and helpful to older patients. Assume an active role in your health care. Research and find ways of improving your health on your own.

10. Take nurturance from our rich cultural heritage as women of wisdom. American women are waking up to realize this has been a patriarchal society for too long.

We need to look at women in other cultures to gain a broader perspective. Most of all, we need to find ways of incorporating the lessons we can learn from cultures that honor both age and older women. Many of us are wiser now than before. Our technological society does not offer us ways to share this wisdom. We must find them.

Women are becoming politicians, writers, spiritual leaders, lawyers, physicians. The role of the grandmother is vital and needs more thought and expansion—not in terms of more baby-sitting, but in more ways to tell our stories and share our insights with the young. The culture needs our input, and we need to give it to fulfill the goals of the second half of life.

11. Learn to mourn your losses and then let go. This will free you to start a new life. Consider your losses—even the contracting of one's life that often accompanies the older years—as stimuli to develop inner growth. Live from the inside out, not the other way around.

12. Avoid the pitfall of your own negative thoughts about aging. Dr. Rose Tennant said, "We can learn, grow, and experience life at any age." Sarah said, "It isn't over 'til you close your eyes!"

OUR CONTRIBUTION TO SOCIETY

Many of the changes we have talked about involve a consideration of the self apart from the culture. Even at times they imply running against the culture when it discounts "older" people. Paradoxically, people in this age group, fifty to seventy-five-plus, traditionally are the ones who are counted on to maintain the culture. They support local symphonies, work on community boards, stand for the ethical principles of the society, dress up like Santa Claus, and bake turkeys to carry on our very personal customs. Throwing out the entire culture would be not only impossible but chaotic. We stand as monitors, letting the country know where we see selfishness, injustice, and corruption. Still, we are there to show our grandchildren how to hang their Christmas stockings.

A woman of fifty-plus starts off in her new phase of life with a handicap. Since life is not a golf game, she will not get extra points or a special allowance. Instead of giving extra encouragement, society will be involved in keeping her out of the game. When employment practices work against her and family pressures may even increase, a woman can feel defeated.

Women of this age grew up unaware of their need to know themselves and to assess their goals. They lived in a world where values were preset and repeated in home, school, and church with a stifling and monotonous consistency. These women usually were not alerted to the presence of other values and the need to search for their own truths. As a result, most of the women I talked with feel a sense of being sold a bill of goods, of being "used" by society. They were told their primary value was in nurturing their husbands and the young. No one asked what they would like, and no one is asking today. The role was assigned to them that no one else wanted—the laundry and the stove. Yet this role is vital, and fortunate is the woman who has found it fulfilling. It is said that the caretaking, homemaking role has been denigrated, and I do not wish to further do so. The point is that women were *assigned* to it. When society accepts the importance of this role, it will be sought by men, and the women who follow it will be honored as they are in China.

At the same time, the needs of middle-aged women are ignored. The needs of young adults are highlighted in many ways, as are the needs of older adults who need caring attention. Government grants and society's focus are now on drug addiction and the management of senility. The middle group of women are supposed to be all set for happy retirement. It is apparent that most of them are far from "set." Too old to get good jobs and too young for Social Security, many are desperate with no real purpose for their lives.

Many women over fifty feel a bit like Rip Van Winkle as they awaken to their own needs and find themselves in a strange world. Today's world emphasizes material goods, success, and power more than the world they remember. Further, it is a new kind of society that conflicts with their basic beliefs. They think raising children is important, that relationships are a core focus of a good life. They find religion central to their belief system.

Younger educated women may prefer careers to children, and families that are created often split apart. A new sexual freedom and a pill that prevents pregnancy have changed the way men and women relate to each other. Religious leaders are jailed for their own corruption. Political leaders are found wanting in basic concern for the family, the unit of our society. Television commercials tout the virtues of youth and physical beauty for women, while gray-haired women peddle laxatives and pads to stop embarrassing urinary flow. Children are abused, crime and violence are on the rise. It is more important to have a BMW than to read good literature. How did it all happen? What can we do about it? It is hard to feel like a stranger in your own country.

The woman who continues to grow adapts some of the power of the Apache Changing Woman. She sees the power of aging, and she develops an increased sense of herself. She recognizes that the adaptability that got her through the Depression, World War II, Vietnam, and the "Me Generation" now can be used to improve her life. With a new sense of dedication to this effort, she reaches out to community resources to help her as she searches for new meaning and purpose.

We need to bring men along with us. Rachel Zane cautions that women are so busy growing and changing, they are leaving men behind. We need to convey our new awareness of life goals, to share our insights, with men. We need to bring them along, not in a militant way but as partners in solving joint concerns. If we don't, we will have another problem. There was a folk song we used to sing as children:

Reuben, Reuben, I've been thinking
What a strange world this would be
If the men were all transported
Far beyond the Northern sea

It would be an easier world in some ways, but lonely.

The aware woman welcomes change. Change is the only thing we can count on. Nothing stays the same. A changing society is open to all ideas, all methods. The new woman over fifty looks for ways to contribute her wisdom to that society.

BIBLIOGRAPHY

Chapter 1 Emily's Birthday Party

Downing, Christine. *Journey through Menopause: A Personal Rite of Passage.* New York: Crossroad Publishing Co., 1987.

Ehrenreich, Barbara, and Deirdre English. *For Her Own Good.* New York: Anchor Books, 1979.

Friedan, Betty. *The Feminine Mystique.* New York: W.W. Norton, 1963.

Gordon, Richard E. *The Split-Level Trap.* New York: Geiss, 1960.

Hewlett, Sylvia Ann. *A Lesser Life.* New York: Wm. Morrow & Co., 1986.

Mintz, Steven, and Susan Kellogg. *Domestic Revolutions.* New York: The Free Press, 1988.

Rosenmayr, Leopold. "Changing Values and Positions of Aging in Western Culture." In Birren, James E., and K. Warner Schaie. *Handbook of the Psychology of Aging.* New York: Van Nostrand Reinhold Co., 1985.

Wylie, Philip. *Generation of Vipers.* New York: Pocketbooks, Inc., 1965.

Chapter 2 The Golden Years?

Anderson, Barbara G. *The Aging Game.* New York: McGraw-Hill, 1979.

Breytspraak, Linda. *The Development of Self in Later Life.* Boston: Little, Brown and Co., 1984.

Cabot, Natalie Harris. *You Can't Count on Dying.* Boston: Houghton Mifflin Co., 1961.

Campbell, Shirley. "The Fifty-Year Old Woman and Midlife Stress." *International Journal of Aging and Human Development* 1983–84, 18(4):295–305.

Carlson, Avis D. *In the Fullness of Time.* Chicago: Contemporary Books, 1977.

Cole, Thomas R. "Aging, Meaning, and Well-Being: Musings of a Cultural Historian." *International Journal of Aging and Human Development* 1984, 19(4).

Huyck, Margaret H. *Growing Older.* New York: Prentice-Hall, 1974.

Lessing, Doris. *The Summer before the Dark.* New York: Bantam, 1973.

Moore, Pat. *Disguised.* Waco, Tex.: World Books, 1985.

Neugarten, Bernice L. "The Rise of the Young Old." In Gross, Ronald, Beatrice Gross, and Sylvia Seidman. *The New Old: Struggling for Decent Aging.* Garden City, N.Y.: Anchor Books, 1978.

Rubin, Lillian. *Women of a Certain Age.* New York: Harper & Row, 1979.

Shanas, Ethel, Ph.D. "Old Parents and Middle-Aged Children: The Four and Five Generation Family." *Journal of Geriatric Psychiatry* 1987:7–19.

Chapter 3 The Power of Aging

American Medical Association. *Health and Well-Being After 50.* New York: Random House, 1984.

Baltimore Longitudinal Study of Aging. Baltimore: U.S. Department of Human Services, National Institute of Health, 1984.

Bengston, Vern L., Margaret N. Reedy, and Chad Gordon. "Aging and Self-Conceptions: Personality Processes and Social Contexts." In Birren, James E., and K. Warner Schaie. *Handbook of the Psychology of Aging.* New York: Van Nostrand Reinhold Co., 1985.

Botwinick, Jack. *Aging and Behavior: A Comprehensive Integration of Research Findings.* New York: Springer Co., 1984.

Brecker, Edward M., ed. *Love, Sex, and Aging: A Consumer's Union Report.* Boston: Little, Brown and Co., 1984.

Brewi, Janice, and Anne Brennan. *Celebrate Mid-Life.* New York: Crossroad Publishing Co., 1988.

Buck, Pearl. *Modern Maturity* 1971, October–November.

Cabot, Natalie Harris. *You Can't Count on Dying*. Boston: Houghton Mifflin Co., 1961.

Carlson, Avis D. *In the Fullness of Time*. Chicago: Contemporary Books, 1977. Quoting Pearl Buck.

Diller, Phyllis. *The Joys of Aging, and How to Avoid Them*. Garden City, N.Y.: Doubleday and Company, Inc., 1981.

Dychtwald, Ken, Ph.D. *Age Wave*. Los Angeles: Jeremy P. Tarcher, Inc., 1989.

Eliot, T.S. *Four Quartets*. New York: Burnt-Norton, 1925.

Erdwins, Carol J., Jeanne C. Mellinger, and Zita E. Tyler. "A Comparison of Different Aspects of Self-Concept for Young, Middle-Aged, and Older Women." *Journal of Clinical Psychology* 1981, 37(3).

Fisher, M.F.K. *Sister Age*. New York: Random House, 1984.

Flach, Frederic, M.D. *Resilience: Discovering a New Strength at Times of Stress*. New York: Fawcett Columbine, 1988.

Fries, James F., and Lawrence M. Crapo. *Vitality and Aging*. New York: W. H. Freeman and Co., 1981.

Fritz, Robert. *The Path of Least Resilience: Learning to Become the Creative Force in Your Own Life*. New York: Ballantine Books, 1989.

Henig, Robin Marantz. *How A Woman Ages*. New York: Esquire Press, 1985.

Jung, Carl, M.D. *Modern Man in Search of a Soul*. San Diego: Harcourt Brace Jovanovich. First published in 1933.

————. "Youth and Age." In *Psychological Reflections*. New York: Harper Torchbooks, 1961.

Labouvie-Vief, Gisela. "Intelligence and Cognition." In Birren, James E., and K. Warner Schaie. *Handbook of the Psychology of Aging*. New York: Van Nostrand Reinhold, 1985.

Lowenathal, Marjorie, Majda Thurnher, and David Chiriboga. *Four Stages of Life*. San Francisco: Jossey-Bass, 1975.

Maslow, Abraham H. *Motivation and Personality*. New York: Harper & Row, 1970.

O'Keeffe, Georgia. In Goodrich, Lloyd, and Doris Bry. *Georgia O'Keeffe*. New York: Praeger, 1970.

Olsen, Tillie. *Silences*. Lawrence, N.Y.: Laurel/Seymour, 1978.

Pfeiffer, Eric, Adrian Verwoerdt, and Glenn Davis. "Sexual Behavior in Middle Life." *American Journal of Psychiatry* 1972, 128(10):1264.

Poon, Leonard W. "Differences in Human Memory with Aging: Nature, Causes, and Clinical Implications." In Birren, James E., and K. Warner Schaie. *Handbook of the Psychology of Aging.* New York: Van Nostrand Reinhold, 1985.

Sarton, May. *At Seventy: A Journal.* New York: W.W. Norton and Company, 1984.

Ward, Russell A. *The Aging Experience: An Introduction to Social Gerontology.* New York: Harper & Row, 1984.

Williams, Redford B., et al. "Type A Behavior and Angiographically Documented Coronary Atherosclerosis in a Sample of 2,289 Patients." *Psychosomatic Medicine* 1988, 50:139–152.

Woolf, Virginia. *A Writer's Life.* New York: W.W. Norton, 1985.

Zeidenstein, Sondra. *A Wider Giving: Women Writing After a Long Silence.* Gosen, Conn.: Chicory Blue Press, 1989.

Vibrator Information

Write to "Good Vibrations," 1210 Valencia St., San Francisco, Calif. Send $2 for catalogue. Low to moderate prices.

Write for information about Dr. Ruth Westheimer's new appliance, the Eroscillator, marketed by the Advanced Response Corporation, P.O. Box 6380, Boca Raton, Florida 33427. More expensive.

Chapter 4 Surviving in a Difficult World

Carnegie, Dale. *How to Win Friends and Influence People,* rev. New York: Pocket Books, 1981.

———. *How to Stop Worrying and Start Living.* New York: Pocket Books, 1984.

———. *The Quick and Easy Way to Effective Speaking.* New York: Pocket Books, 1962.

Pearlin, Leonard I., and Carmi Schooler. "The Structure of Coping." *Journal of Health and Social Behavior* March 2–21, 1978, 19:2–21.

Reflecting Elsie's Philosophy

Moss, Richard, M.D. *The I That Is We: Awakening to Higher Energies Through Unconditional Love.* Berkeley: Celestial Arts, 1981.

Chapter 5 The Inward Journey

Bach, George R., M.D., and Laura Torbet. *The Inner Enemy*. New York: William Morrow and Company, 1983.

Beattie, Melody. *Co-Dependent No More*. New York: Harper & Row, 1987.

Beck, Aaron T., M.D. *Cognitive Therapy and the Emotional Disorders*. New York: New American Library, Inc., 1976.

Benson, Herbert, et al. "Historical and Clinical Considerations of the Relaxation Response." *American Scientist* 1977, 65(4):441–445.

Bloomfield, Harold H., M.D. *Making Peace with Your Parents*. New York: Random House, 1983.

Borysenko, Joan, Ph.D. *Minding the Body, Mending the Mind*. Reading, Mass.: Addison-Wesley, 1987.

Brewi, Janice, and Anne Brennan. *Celebrate Mid-Life*. New York: Crossroad Publishing Co., 1988.

Breytspraak, Linda M. *The Development of Self in Later Life*. Boston: Little, Brown and Co., 1984.

Burns, David D., M.D. *Feeling Good*. New York: New American Library, 1980.

Calvert, Judi. "Mary Burmeister: World's Leading Authority and Teacher of the Art of Jin Shin Jyutsu—The Simple Art of Living." *Massage Magazine* Aug./Sept. 1989.

Dreher, Henry. "The Perspectives and Programs of Behavioral Medicine." *Advances* 1986, 3(1).

Erickson, Erik. *Adulthood*. New York: W.W. Norton, 1978.

Felder, Leonard. "How to Handle Your Success." *Writer's Digest*, August 1988.

Fensterheim, Herbert, Ph.D. *Don't Say Yes When You Want to Say No*. New York: David McKay Company, 1975.

Friedan, Betty. *The Feminine Mystique*. New York: W.W. Norton, 1963.

Harris, Jean. *Stranger in Two Worlds*. New York: Kensington Publishing Corp., 1986.

Hay, Louise. *Love Your Body*. Santa Monica: Hay House, Inc., 1988.

Jencks, Beata, Ph.D. *Your Body: Biofeedback at Its Best*. Chicago: Nelson-Hall, 1977.

Leonard, Linda Schierse. *The Wounded Woman*. Boston: Shambhala Publications, 1985.

Norwood, Robin. *Women Who Love Too Much.* Los Angeles: Jeremy Tarcher, 1985.

Orme-Johnson, Ph.D. "Medical Care Utilization and the Transcendental Meditation Program." *Psychosomatic Medicine* 1987, 49:493–507.

Ornstein, Robert, Ph.D., and David Sobel, M.D. *Healthy Pleasures.* Reading, Mass.: Addison-Wesley Publishing Co., 1989.

Pollock, George H., M.D., Ph.D. "The Psychoanalytic Treatment of Older Adults with Special Reference to the Mourning-Liberation Process." *Current Psychiatric Therapies* 1986:87–98.

Shapiro, David, Ph.D., and Gary Schwartz, Ph.D. "Biofeedback and Visceral Learning: Clinical Applications." *Seminars in Psychiatry* 1972, 4(2).

Sheehan, George, M.D. *This Running Life.* New York: Simon and Schuster, 1980.

Squires, Sally. "Vision to Boost Immunity." *American Health,* July 1987. Contains research of Dr. Joan Borysenko.

White, E.B. "To Catherine S. White." In *The Letters of E.B. White.* New York: Harper & Row, 1976.

Self-Esteem Audiotapes

Branden, Nathaniel, Ph.D. *Experience Self-Esteem.* Sound Ideas, Simon and Schuster, 1988.

Erickson, Carol. *Natural Self-Confidence.* Ericksonian Hypnosis. Changeworks, P.O. Box 4000-D, Berkeley, CA.

Hay, Louise L., and Joshua Leeds. *Songs of Affirmation.* Santa Monica: Hay House, Inc.

Hay, Louise. *Conversations on Living.* Santa Monica: Hay House, Inc., 1987.

Self-Esteem Books

Barksdale, L.S. *Essays on Self-Esteem.* The Barksdale Foundation, Idyllwild, Calif., 1977. Also available on audiotape.

Briggs, Dorothy Corkille. *Celebrate Yourself.* New York: Bantam Doubleday Bell, 1977.

Christopherson, Pat. *Feeling Good About Feeling Bad.* Rapid City, S.D.: Golden Egg Publishing, 1987.

Hendricks, Gay, Ph.D. *Learning to Love Yourself.* New York: Prentice-Hall, 1982.

McKay, Matthew, Ph.D, and Patricia Fenning. *Self-Esteem: A Study of Cognitive Techniques.* Oakland: New Harbinger Publications, 1987.

Sandord, Linda, and Mary Ellen Donovan. *Women and Self-Esteem.* Penguin Books, 1985.

Satir, Virginia. *Self-Esteem.* Berkeley: Celestial Arts, 1975.

Simmermacher, Donald. *Self-Image Modification.* Deerfield Beach, Fla.: Health Communications, 1981.

Chapter 6 Reaching Out to the World

Bolles, R.N. *The Three Boxes of Life.* Berkeley: Ten Speed Press, 1978.

Brewi, Janice, and Anne Brennan. *Celebrate Mid-Life.* New York: Crossroad Publishing Co., 1988.

Buckley, Joe. *The Retirement Handbook.* New York: Harper & Row, 1977.

Jones, Warren H., Stephen Briggs, and Jonathan M. Cheek. *Shyness: Perspectives on Research and Treatment.* New York: Plenum Press, 1986.

Sutherland, Louise. *The Impossible Ride.* London: Southern Cross Press, 1982.

Weinland, James D. *How to Improve Your Memory.* Savage, Md.: Barnes and Noble, 1985.

Zarit, Steven H. *Aging and Mental Disorders: Psychological Approaches to Assessment and Treatment.* New York: The Free Press, 1980.

Zimbardo, Philip G. *Shyness.* Reading, Mass.: Addison-Wesley Publishing Co., 1977.

Chapter 7 Older Women in the Business World

Bales, Susan Nall. "Fragments of Time: The Perils of Part-Time Work." *The Owl Observer.* Washington, D.C.: The Older Women's League, 1989.

Bolles, R.N. *What Color Is Your Parachute?* Berkeley: Ten Speed Press, 1983.

Brandt, Ellen. "Secrets of Success after Sixty." *Parade Magazine,* December 13, 1987.

Davidson, Janice. *Employment Concerns of Older Women.* Baltimore: University of Maryland, 1983.

DeGooyer, Janice. *Women, Work, and Age Discrimination.* Washington, D.C.: National Commission on Working Women, 1980.

Meier, Elizabeth. *Employment Experience and Income of Older Women.* 1986.

Myers, Albert, and Christopher Anderson. *Success Over Sixty.* New York: Summit Books, 1984.

Social Insecurity: The Economic Marginalization of Older Workers. Cleveland: Report by 9 to 5, National Association of Working Women, Sept. 1987.

Information on Starting a New Business

The Institute for Success Over Sixty, Box 160, Aspen, Colo., 81612. Newsletter and seminars. Phone: 1-303-925-1900.

New Career Opportunities, Inc., P.O. Box 10366, Glendale, Calif., 91209.

The Service Corps of Retired Executives (SCORE). Look in local telephone directory under U.S. Government-Small Business Administration; or call toll-free: 1-800-368-5855.

Chapter 8 Special Relationships

Anderson, Barbara Gallatin. *The Aging Game.* New York: McGraw-Hill, 1979.

Atchley, R.C., and S.J. Miller. "Types of Elderly Couples." In Brubaker, T. H. *Family Relationships in Later Life.* Beverly Hills, Calif.: Sage, 1983.

Beck, Aaron T. *Love Is Never Enough.* New York: Harper & Row, 1988.

Bloomfield, Harold H., M.D. *Making Peace with Your Parents.* New York: Random House, 1983.

Bramson, Robert, Ph.D. *How to Deal with Difficult People.* New York: Ballantine Books, 1981.

Chekhov, Anton. "The Bear." In Morris Sweetkind, editor. *Ten Great One Act Plays.* New York: Bantam, 1968.

Dychtwald, Ken, Ph.D. *Age Wave.* Los Angeles: Jeremy P. Tarcher, Inc., 1989.

Flax, Carol C., Ph.D., and Earl Ubell. *Getting Your Way—The Nice Way: A Guide for Parents and Grown-up Children.* Wideview Books, 1982.

Friedman, Roslyn, and Annette Nussbaum. *Coping with Your Husband's Retirement.* New York: Simon and Schuster, 1986.

LeShan, Eda. *Oh, To Be Fifty Again.* New York: Times Books, 1986.

Nussbaum, Jon F., Teresa Thompson, and James D. Robinson. *Communication and Aging.* New York: Harper & Row, 1989.

Robinson, Betsy, Ph.D., and Majda Thurnher, Ph.D. "Taking Care of Aged Parents: A Family Cycle Transition." In *The Gerontologist.* From a paper presented at the 29th Annual Scientific Meeting of the Gerontological Society, New York, October 1976.

Thatcher, Floyd, and Harriett Thatcher. *Long-Term Marriage: A Search for the Ingredients of a Lifetime Partnership.* Waco, Tex.: Word Books, 1980.

Willi, Jurg, M.D. *Couples in Collusion.* Claremont, Calif.: Hunter House, 1982.

Willing, Jules Z. *The Reality of Retirement.* New York: Morrow Quill Paperbacks, 1981.

Zarit, Stephen H. *Aging and Mental Disorders: Psychological Approaches to Assessment and Treatment.* New York: The Free Press, 1980.

[*The author regrets not giving proper credit for some of the suggestions on pages 181–182; she was unable to track down her original source.*]

Chapter 9 Relating to Our Doctors

Current Therapy. Philadelphia: Saunders, annually.

Dychtwald, Ken. Interviewed in Michael Shrange, "Old Age Evangelist." In *Special Report.* Knoxville: Whittle Communications, April 1989:47.

Gafner, George, M.S.W. "Engaging the Elderly Couple in Marital Therapy." *The American Journal of Family Therapy* 1987, 15(4).

Index Medicus. Bethesda, Md.: National Institute of Health, annually.

Kübler-Ross, Elisabeth, M.D. In Zarit, Stephen H. *Aging and Mental Disorders.* New York: The Free Press, 1980.

Matthews, Dale A., M.D. "I Wish I'd Known She Loved Chopin." *Senior Patient,* March/April 1989.

Physicians Desk Reference. Oradell, N.J.: Medical Economics Co., annually.

Zarit, Steven H. *Aging and Mental Disorders: Psychological Approaches to Assessment and Treatment*. New York: The Free Press, 1980.

Chapter 10 Reclaiming Our Heritage

Alexander, Hartley Burr. *The World's Rim: Great Mysteries of the North American Indians*. Lincoln, Neb.: University of Nebraska Press, 1953.

Allione, Tsultrim. *Women of Wisdom*. New York: Routledge and Kegan Paul, 1986.

Basson, Keith H. *The Cibecue Apache*. New York: Holt, Rinehart, and Winston, 1970.

Brown, Judith K., and Virginia Kerns. *In Her Prime: A New View of Middle-Aged Women*. South Hadley, Mass.: Bergin and Garvey, 1985.

Gray, Elizabeth Dodson. *Sacred Dimensions of Women's Experience*. Wellesley, Mass.: Roundtable Press, 1988.

Gutmann, David. "The Cross-Cultural Perspective: Notes Toward a Comparative Psychology on Aging." In Birren, James E., and K. Warner Schaie. *Handbook of the Psychology of Aging*. New York: Van Nostrand Reinhold Co., 1985.

Lau, Elizabeth. *Innovative Parenting*. Hong Kong: Sun Ya Publishing Co., 1980. (In Chinese.)

Neithammer, Carolyn. *Daughters of the Earth*. New York: Macmillan, 1977.

Steiger, Brad. *American Indian Magic: Sacred Powwows and Hopi Prophecies*. New Brunswick, N.J.: Inner Light Publications, 1986.

Stone, Merlin. *When God Was a Woman*. San Diego: Harcourt Brace Jovanovich, 1976.

Walker, Barbara F. *The Crone: A Woman of Age, Wisdom, and Power*. San Francisco: Harper & Row, 1985.

Ywahoo, Dhyami. *Voices of Our Ancestors: Cherokee Teachings from the Wisdom Fire*. Boston: Shambhala Publications, 1987.

Chapter 11 Reflections

Buck, Pearl S. Quoted from *Modern Maturity* Oct.–Nov. 1971. In Carlson, Avis D. *In the Fullness of Time*. Contemporary Books, Chicago, 1977.

Butler, R.N. "The Life Review: An Interpretation of Reminiscence in the Aged." In Neugarten, Bernice L. *Middle Age and Aging*. Chicago: The University of Chicago Press, 1968.

Capacchione, Lucia, M.A. *The Creative Journal: The Art of Finding Yourself*. North Hollywood, Calif.: Newcastle Publishing Co., 1989.

Neugarten, Bernice L. "Inner-Life Processes." In Huyck, Margaret Hellie. *Growing Older*. New York: Prentice-Hall, 1974.

Praeger, Dennis. "What Makes a Happy Person?" *Redbook* 172 (Feb. 1989), 76–77.

Progoff, Ira. *At a Journal Workshop*. New York: Dialogue House Library, 1975.

Scott-Maxwell, Florida. *The Measure of My Days*. New York: Knopf, 1968.